Russell and Wittgenstein on the Nature of Judgement

Continuum Studies in British Philosophy

Series Editor: James Fieser, University of Tennessee at Martin

Berkeley and Irish Philosophy – David Berman
Bertrand Russell's Ethics – Michael K. Potter
Boyle on Fire – William Eaton
Coherence of Hobbes's Leviathan – Eric Brandon
Doing Austin Justice – Wilfrid Rumble
The Early Wittgenstein on Religion – J. Mark Lazenby
Francis Bacon and the Limits of Scientific Knowledge – Dennis Desroches
Hume's Theory of Causation – Angela Coventry
Idealist Political Philosophy – Colin Tyler
John Stuart Mill's Political Philosophy – John Fitzpatrick
Popper, Objectivity and the Growth of Knowledge – John H. Sceski
Rethinking Mill's Ethics – Colin Heydt
Russell and Wittgenstein on the Nature of Judgement – Rosalind Carey
Russell's Theory of Perception – Sajahan Miah
Thomas Hobbes and the Politics of Natural Philosophy – Stephen J. Finn
Thomas Reid's Ethics – William C. Davis
Wittgenstein and the Theory of Perception – Justin Good
Wittgenstein at His Word – Duncan Richter
Wittgenstein's Religious Point of View – Tim Labron

Russell and Wittgenstein on the Nature of Judgement

Rosalind Carey

continuum

Continuum International Publishing Group
The Tower Building, 11 York Road, London SE1 7NX
80 Maiden Lane, Suite 704, New York NY 10038

www.continuumbooks.com

British Library Cataloguing-in-Publication Data
A catalogue record for this book is available from the British Library.

ISBN-10: HB: 0-8264-8811-0
ISBN-13: 978-0-8264-8811-4

Library of Congress Cataloging-in-Publication Data
Carey, Rosalind.
    Russell and Wittgenstein on the nature of judgement / by Rosalind Carey.
        p. cm.
    Includes bibliographical references (p.   ) and index.
        ISBN-13: 978-0-8264-8811-4
        ISBN-10: 0-8264-8811-0
    1. Judgment.   2.   Russell, Bertrand, 1872–1970.   3.   Wittgenstein, Ludwig,
1889–1951.   I. Title.

    B1649.R94C38 2007
    192–dc22

2006038316

Typeset by Kenneth Burnley, Wirral, Cheshire
Printed and bound in Great Britain by Biddles Ltd, King's Lynn, Norfolk

Contents

	List of Figures	vii
	Introduction	1
1	The Origin and Development of the Multiple Relation Theory of Judgement	11
2	The Nature of the Proposition	42
3	Analysis, Belief, Truth and Certainty	70
4	The Form of Belief	94
	Appendix	115
	Notes	121
	Bibliography	137
	Index	147

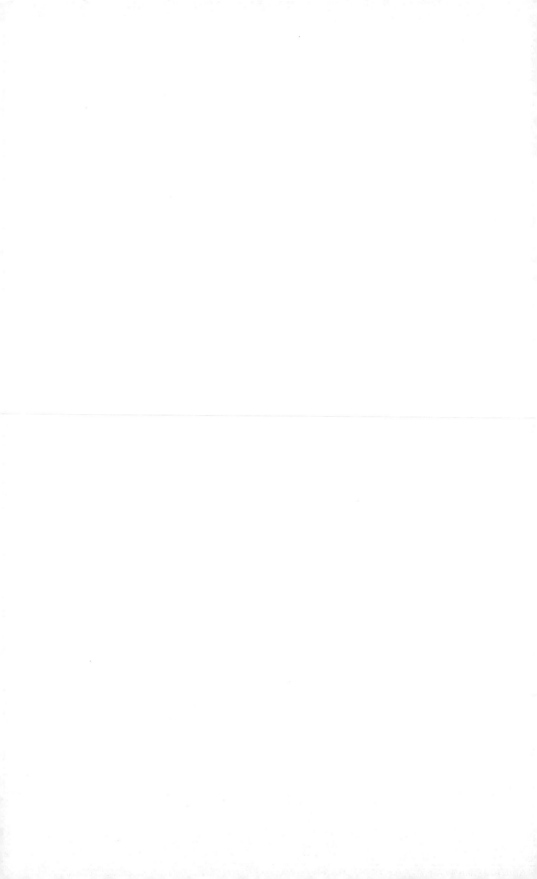

Figures

1   Composing the *Theory of Knowledge*   5

2   Diagram of judgement (without form)   60

3   Diagram in *Theory of Knowledge* of understanding
(with form)   65

4   Early draft of the diagram of understanding   66

5   Diagram in 'Props' of understanding   103

6   Diagram in 'Props' of the bipolarity of judging   104

7   Wittgenstein's diagram in 'Notes on Logic' of the
poles of a proposition   104

8   Russell's 1918 diagram of bipolarity   105

Introduction

[Wittgenstein's criticism was] an event of first rate importance in my life, and affected everything I have done since . . . I saw he was right, and I saw that I could not hope ever again to do fundamental work in philosophy . . . I *had* to produce lectures for America, but I took a metaphysical subject although I was and am convinced that all fundamental work in philosophy is logical. My reason was that Wittgenstein persuaded me that what wanted doing in logic was too difficult for me.[1] (Russell to Ottoline, 1916)

Introduction

In 1911, not long after Russell completes the *Principia Mathematica*[2] and begins to direct his energies to new projects, Wittgenstein and Russell begin their brief but historically formative interchanges about the nature of logic and cognition.[3] Impressed by his student's character and strength of mind,[4] Russell begins casting Wittgenstein as the one to carry on the work of solving the remaining flaws in the *Principia*,[5] and his prediction that Wittgenstein will set right the flaws in *Principia* begins to unfold in a devastating way in 1913.[6] The context is his work on a new book, the *Theory of Knowledge*, which Russell hopes will lay out the epistemological doctrines sketched in *Principia*. His work on the text begins on 7 May, and in between then and early June he churns out chapters or portions of chapters only to be periodically interrupted by Wittgenstein, who first appears to express disapproval at the epistemological project in general,[7] and who then appears with a series of objections to a central doctrine in the book. The focus of Wittgenstein's attack is Russell's so-called multiple relation theory of judgement, a doctrine on which a subject

A is related to the objects (a, R, b) of her belief by a polyadic relation *judging*. Though Russell seems to have suspected, if not fully grasped, the seriousness of the difficulties facing him soon after Wittgenstein began voicing them, he doesn't immediately abandon the manuscript. But in mid-June, two days after a meeting with Wittgenstein that comes on the heels of a letter in which Wittgenstein states objections to Russell's theory of judgement,[8] Russell confides to Ottoline that Wittgenstein has made his work 'impossible for years to come'.[9] Not long after, Wittgenstein writes to express sympathy for the fact that his objections have 'paralysed' Russell.[10]

The ideas contained in the 1913 manuscript are never mentioned in Russell's later work. Indeed, his silence concerning the 1913 manuscript was so complete that the manuscript's existence remained unknown until 1967. Then, to raise money for the International War Crimes Tribunal, the 95-year-old Bertrand Russell sold a bundle of manuscripts, including one large, unfamiliar one, to the Russell Archives at McMaster University. The archivists wrote back to Russell concerning the large manuscript dating from 1913 and clearly of some importance, but Russell did not reply to their queries, dying soon after at the age of 97.

The Nature of the Question and the Evidence

Though Russell abandons the manuscript, he continues to defend and develop new versions of the multiple relation theory long afterwards, and hence the present text asks: what objections to his theory of judgement could have allowed Russell to think his theory of judgement was still viable but sufficed to cause him to abandon the manuscript? To find an answer to this question is the goal of the present text, but to understand the objections, Russell's way of construing them, and his attempts to accommodate them in the texts we would like to be privy to a first-hand discussion of the conversations, and given Russell's silence on the matter for the most part we are not. A great deal of the information we have on the events of this period is in the form of private letters; that we possess any information at all is largely due to Russell's habit of writing daily to his companion Ottoline Morrell. The letters provide data on the sequence of Russell's work on the *Theory of Knowledge*, i.e. which chapter he is completing, what he plans to turn to next, and so on; and they also indicate in some cases down to the hour when Wittgenstein visits his chambers to deliver objections and criticisms to the emerging manuscript.

Besides the above information, the letters provide a general sense of Wittgenstein's objections and Russell's reaction to them; as noted above, Wittgenstein appears to have focused on flaws in Russell's theory of belief (judgement) and his analysis of propositions. Yet what the letters don't provide is a clear sense of what exactly Wittgenstein found so distressing in Russell's analysis of belief and to what extent and in what way Russell plans to accommodate those objections in the pages he subsequently drafts. The lack of clarity is only partly because Russell's letters to Ottoline are personal and his references to Wittgenstein's objections are correspondingly brief and general. The difficulty of discerning Wittgenstein's objections from Russell's letters is equally due to Wittgenstein's inarticulateness – Russell objects to this himself – and it is worth keeping in mind that Russell's letters (and the *Theory of Knowledge* itself) record both Russell's and Wittgenstein's struggle to understand Wittgenstein's objections.[11]

The obscurity of many of Russell's and Wittgenstein's letters may seem to present an insurmountable obstacle to achieving a good picture of the events leading up to the collapse of Russell's new project. But the situation is not as grim as might at first seem. Besides Russell's and Wittgenstein's letters we possess the *Theory of Knowledge*, numerous notes and diagrams Russell composed while drafting the text, as well as Russell's earlier and later writings and Wittgenstein's notes. The manuscript and notes exhibit Russell's responses to Wittgenstein's objections. In addition, Russell's work after 1913 provides further evidence. In that later work Russell explicitly acknowledges his student's ideas as informing his own thought (how well Russell understands them is another matter) and continues to grapple with the problems Wittgenstein poses in 1913. Though it is open to debate how long Wittgenstein sets the questions for Russell, there can be little doubt that Russell's later attributions to Wittgenstein as well as the nature of the tasks he sets himself shed light on the dark period of the *Theory of Knowledge* when read alongside the documents from that period.

The present text aims to use the above sources to reconstruct the events in this period of Russell's life, to address what Wittgenstein found objectionable in Russell's text and how, in composing the *Theory of Knowledge*, Russell attempts to accommodate what he thinks are Wittgenstein's criticisms. The reconstruction will, I hope, also help to clarify Russell's doctrines and concerns in his work following 1913, showing how they emerge from his conversation with Wittgenstein in 1913.

Which Chapters Show Signs of Wittgenstein's Impact?

What Russell wanted to achieve in the *Theory of Knowledge* and how far he actually gets provide important clues as to the nature of his dialogue with Wittgenstein. The book focuses on an analysis of experience into such data as a particular patch of colour or one sound following another, classifying data in terms of the kinds of (direct or complex) relationships subjects have to what they experience. As we know from notes found with the manuscript and laying out his anticipated chapters, the book was to contain an analytic section and a constructive section.[12] The third and final section of the analytic half of the book and the entire constructive half are never written. In the analytic half of the book, Russell defends a Cartesian dualism of mind and matter by means of an analysis of the kind of one-on-one, unmediated relation the mind has to objects in perceiving and attending to them. He then shows how his dualism, whose foundation is the defence of simple, direct relations between minds and things, is consistent with an account of relations between the mind and the world that are not direct or 'dual'. That is, he explains how a mind, in understanding, believing, or willing, stands in a complex relation to a complex of things.

The analytic part of the *Theory of Knowledge* was supposed to give a complete analysis of experience by moving from simple forms of experience to more complex kinds, that is, by moving from acquaintance to belief and then to inference. In fact, after completing the section on acquaintance, Russell revises his outline so as to move from acquaintance to atomic propositions and then to molecular ones. He completes only the analysis of acquaintance and atomic propositional thought (parts I and II), and abandons his manuscript at the point of transition to the analysis of molecular propositions. Some discussion of themes belonging to the section on molecular propositions is anticipated in his treatment of earlier themes, and it is in part his sense of the difficulties Wittgenstein has stirred up for an analysis of these topics that, I believe, led Russell to believe that completion of the project to be out of reach.

Figure 1 displays the book's chapters and the dates they were drafted; the dates on which Wittgenstein levelled his objections are shown in **bold**.

Part I	On the Nature of Acquaintance	
Chapter 1	Preliminary Description of Experience	7 May
Chapter 2	Neutral Monism	9 May
Chapter 3	Analysis of Experience	11–13 May
Chapter 4	Definitions and Method. Principles . . .	
Chapter 5	Sensation and . . .	14 May
Chapter 6	On the Experience of Time	17–19 May
	[Russell takes a day off: **20** May]	
Chapter 7	On the Acquaintance . . . of Relations	21 May
Chapter 8	Acquaintance . . . Predicates	**23** May
Chapter 9	Logical Data	
Part II	Atomic Propositional Thought	
Chapter 1	The Understanding of Propositions	24–**26** May
Chapter 2	Analysis and Synthesis	27 May
Chapter 3	Various Examples of Understanding	28–29 May
Chapter 4	Belief, Disbelief, and Doubt	30 May
Chapter 5	Truth and Falsehood	31 May
Chapter 6	Self-Evidence	5 June
Chapter 7	Degrees of Certainty	6 June

Figure 1. *Composing the* Theory of Knowledge

What follows the demise of the *Theory of Knowledge* is outside the scope of the present book, at least as a matter for direct inquiry. Months after the demise of the book, Russell begins to prepare chapters 1–6 of the *Theory of Knowledge* for publication, revising only chapter 4. Though an exact date is unknown, the revision may coincide with the transcription of Wittgenstein's *Notes on Logic* in early October 1913. The revised chapter contains Russell's first footnote to Wittgenstein.[13]

After recording the *Notes on Logic*, Wittgenstein moves to Norway to write. Despite the fact that the onset of World War I severs his communication with Wittgenstein,[14] Russell continues to respond to Wittgenstein's objections, articulating influential doctrines that are increasingly scientific in orientation but have their origin in his 1913 conversations with Wittgenstein.

The Contents of the Chapters in this Text

Wittgenstein's objections to Russell's theory of judgement come in three waves: the first occurs on 20 May, the second on 26 May, and the third and final one in mid-June, as recorded in his letter to Russell. The nature of his objections as well as the nature of Russell's response forms the core of three of the four chapters of this study. The topic of Chapter 1 prefaces the issues dealt with in those chapters by looking back to the origin and development of the theory of judgement and focusing on Russell's epistemological and logical doctrines in the transitional period between 1903 and 1910. My point in so doing is not simply to present Russell's theory of belief and perception prior to Wittgenstein's impact, to make his influence on the theory easier to detect; rather, my aim is to show how the multiple relation theory of judgement emerges from and is influenced by a number of problems and doctrines that contribute to his eventual paralysis in the face of Wittgenstein's additional objections. Russell's study of Meinong's theory of mind, his attempts to overcome the Liar paradox and his invention of the theory of incomplete symbols are perhaps the most important doctrines to influence and shape his theory of judgement. In discussing how these strands are interwoven I draw attention to the fact that in this period Russell employs the concept of belief in several different ways, all of which contribute to and inform the mature (1910 and later) multiple relation theory. How Russell joins the mature theory to his theory of mind or consciousness to define truth as well as our knowledge of truth is another theme of the first chapter.

Chapter 2 considers the impact of Wittgenstein on Russell's work in 1913 between 20 May and 26 May. On my reconstruction of the conversation on the 20th, Wittgenstein presses Russell to explain how his view of judgement as a kind of fact, a relation of objects, can account for the existence of a proposition or sense, that is, something we understand even when the belief is false. Russell responds, I believe, in two ways: by manipulating the notion of form, and, more ambitiously, by deciding that the second and third parts of his text will focus not on belief and inference, respectively, but on atomic and molecular forms of propositions.

Wittgenstein responds rather violently to Russell's efforts when, on the 26th, he sees some of the work Russell has just completed; and Russell's efforts to maintain his momentum on the *Theory of Knowledge*, while working out a response to Wittgenstein's criticism is the topic of Chapter 3. The chapters covered bring us to the end of the book and include Russell's explanations of the nature of analysis, of belief and disbelief, and of truth, understood in terms of a correspondence between a proposition and a fact. Part of the function of Chapter 3 is to exhibit Russell's growing anxiety over the theories he has just outlined, for it is at this point, that is, after Wittgenstein's angry visit on the 26th, that he begins to grasp the many difficulties affecting his theory of judgement.

Chapter 4 contains a discussion of Wittgenstein's devastating June letter to Russell; in addition to using this letter, my interpretation of why Russell abandons the manuscript comes from examining Russell's notes from this period. I argue that these notes and the diagrams in them contain Russell's final attempt to correct his theory of belief in light of Wittgenstein's outcry on 26 May. The notes in question attempt to account for the sense and bipolarity of propositions by means of a new theory of belief. Though, as he admits, these notes do not resolve the difficulties adequately, they show that Russell did in fact have a fair idea of Wittgenstein's point – despite his remark to Ottoline on the 26th that Wittgenstein was very unclear – and that he believes that belief is a new form, outside the hierarchy of molecular forms. It is this realization that he later expresses when, revising Chapter 4 of the *Theory of Knowledge* for publication, he writes:

> It can be shown that . . . all thought whose expression involves propositions must be a fact of a different form. What is the form of proposition in case of belief: more complicated forms of *p*.[15]

A theme running throughout the chapters of the present text is Russell's Cartesian mind/matter dualism; in particular, his atomism of meaning, his doctrine of an experiencing subject and his theory of perception. In addition to holding that in perceiving we apprehend types of objects, that these are the meanings of words and that sentence meaning emerges from their combination, Russell takes cognitive relations like *judging, asserting* and *perceiving* to be essential to an account of a proposition or sense.[16] Since he holds that the meaning of the names in a sentence correspond to the simples in a complex, he maintains an intensionalist view of meaning on which two sentences that are true or false under exactly the same conditions are nevertheless different in meaning.

Wittgenstein, I believe, urges Russell to reconsider all these notions: the idea that perception can give us type differences, that a proposition is dependent on psychological acts or stands in relation to purported mental entities, and the perspective on which there are distinctions of meaning over and above a proposition's truth-conditions.[17] By pressing Russell to adopt criteria of individuation that do not allow propositions with the same truth conditions to differ in meaning, Wittgenstein also calls into question Russell's view of the logical subject, the one who judges. As I argue in the following pages, Wittgenstein is pressing on Russell that, in the sense relevant to logic, belief is not a particular fact in which there is a(n attitudinal) relation relating a thinker to a proposition. It is natural to wonder whether Wittgenstein's objections had any impact on Russell's 1918 rejection of mind/matter dualism, but this question is one that I merely raise and cannot answer in the following chapters.

Framed in terms of Wittgenstein's concerns, the issues in this study can be described as follows. Already by 1913 Wittgenstein focuses on whatever it is that judgements (thoughts, perceptions, propositional signs, etc.) have in common that allows them to depict a sense and express a thought. In so doing, I think, Wittgenstein is pressing to find a proposition – what is believed – of concern to logic and independent of psychological conditions like judging, asserting and negating. In his 1913 'Notes on Logic', Wittgenstein says:

> However, for instance, 'not-p' may be explained, the question of what is negated must have a meaning.[18]

Russell's doctrine of belief attempts to make an occurrence or fact of belief (a relation like *believing*) responsible for what is believed, a proposition with a sense. Against Russell's conception, Wittgenstein writes:

> Judgement, question, and command are all on the same level. What interests logic in them is only the unasserted proposition.[19]

Wittgenstein insists, against Russell, that a proposition is presupposed by mental acts of judging, perceiving, etc. and does not presuppose these acts. It is presumably this sense in which Wittgenstein remarks in the *Tractatus* that propositions are 'logically completely in order'.[20]

In conveying these ideas to Russell, Wittgenstein shows a preoccupation with the presuppositions of any kind of depiction, that is, with what might be called the logic of depiction. This emphasis has an important consequence: it highlights the kind of evidence underlying philosophical judgements, i.e. the kind of evidence underlying propositions asserting, for example, the nature of relations. On Wittgenstein's view, such purported propositions attempt to say what cannot be said, but is instead shown by assertions' having certain structures. Whether or not Wittgenstein has already begun to view metaphysical assertions as nonsensical ones and to view language as misleading us by giving nonsensical assertions the appearance of sense, his push to find what is essential to depicting comes across very powerfully and is important in shaping Russell's responses to Wittgenstein in the parts of the *Theory of Knowledge* under discussion in this text.

Chapter 1

The Origin and Development of the Multiple Relation Theory of Judgement

The theory of knowledge is often regarded as identical with logic. This view results from confounding psychical states with their objects; for, when it is admitted that the proposition known is not identical with the knowledge of it, it becomes plain that the question as to the nature of propositions is distinct from all questions of knowledge . . . The theory of knowledge is in fact distinct from psychology, but is more complex: for it involves not only what psychology has to say about belief, but also the distinction of truth and falsehood, since knowledge is only belief in what is true.[1]

Introduction

Othello believes that Desdemona loves Cassio. His belief has meaning – it expresses a proposition – but how? What is the nature of judging? What is the nature of a proposition? On Russell's multiple relation theory, in Othello's act of judging (believing) that Desdemona loves Cassio the relation *judging* appropriately groups the objects of Othello's belief – Cassio, *loves* and Desdemona – plus Othello himself into a complex or fact. In 1910 Russell says of the event of judging:

> At the time when I judge, there is a certain complex whose terms are myself and A and loves and B, and whose relating relation is *judging*.[2]

The so-called multiple relation theory is perhaps not the most intuitive account of the nature of judging, and it is not immediately obvious why Russell should adopt it. Why Russell did so is the topic of this chapter. Or rather, I draw attention in this chapter to the most important elements contributing to his decision to adopt the theory, for what will become apparent in the following pages is that he doesn't embrace the doctrine of judgement as a (multiple) relation all at once, nor do so in a uniform way, but develops various versions of the theory over a period of many years under numerous pressures and alongside other changes in his philosophy. The first important factor in the emergence of the multiple relation theory and discussed in the following is Russell's defence of a quite different view of judgement in his earliest philosophy. At this earlier stage in his thinking (1900–1904/05) judging is not a multiple relation among objects but a direct relation between a self or subject and an extra-mental object, the proposition. This early view is a product of his several assumptions about the nature of meaning, e.g. that meanings are the entities corresponding to words, that each word in a sentence has meaning and that the meaning of a whole sentence presupposes the meaning of its constituent words. On this atomistic doctrine of meaning, propositions are complexes of entities, e.g. the-death-of-Caesar corresponding to sentences, e.g. 'Caesar died'. Another contributing factor in the emergence of his new theory of belief is his conception of logic. In this early period not only do sentences derive meaning from the properties and things in the world, sentences – all sentences, including those of logic and sentences analysing other sentences – are verified by properties in the world. If we ask, 'what kind of knowledge is needed in order to know the truth or falsity of propositions that analyse other propositions?' and 'what is the nature of our knowledge of logical truths?' Russell's answer in this period is 'a species of knowledge of abstract entities'. Thus Russell's conceives of logical propositions as completely general truths about the world, a Platonist conception of logic on which the principles of reasoning are objective, unconditionally true, and immediately applicable to all branches of knowledge. On this view logic is a universal framework within which all reasoning is and must be carried out, and every truth presupposed by logic is therefore counted as a part of logic. These assumptions lead to various difficulties that result, as I show below, in the adoption of a theory of incomplete symbols, by means of which Russell eliminates the need to assume the existence of single 'objective propositions', paving the way for a new account of propositions that reduces them to objects, united with a subject in acts of judging. The ways in which he uses belief, the paradoxes that motivate him to employ belief instead of single propositions and the problems a doctrine of belief poses, form another strand in this chapter, overlapping with my discussion of his introduction of the doctrine of incomplete symbols.

The Emergence of the Theory of Incomplete Symbols

The conception of meaning and logic I note above results in characteristic difficulties. In Russell's 1903 *Principles of Mathematics*, for example, a subject or self who judges that Desdemona loves Cassio is in a direct, dyadic relation with the (true or false) proposition that Desdemona-loves-Cassio. According to Russell's ontological views at that time, every word in a sentence refers to or denotes an entity which is its meaning. A proposition is that complex of meanings, in particular, of things and concepts, whose structure corresponds to the structure of subject term and predicate or verb in a sentence which expresses that proposition. Subject terms refer to things, predicates to concepts, yet, importantly, Russell held that some (though not all) entities could shift position within a complex and remain the same. The concept *red*, for example – the denotation of the predicate 'red' as a predicate – is the same entity whether we refer to it by applying 'red' as a predicate to a thing or treat the concept *red* as the thing or subject we talk about. According to Russell, it must be the case that one underlying item remains the same and has dual roles, one as concept, one as thing, because we cannot intelligibly *say* the terms 'red' as subject and 'red' as predicate differ without being able to treat the predicate as a subject and vice versa, hence without treating them as the same. This is a problem of expressibility, for any attempt to express the difference between 'red' as subject and 'red' as predicate is self-contradictory, it breaks down. Russell, persuaded of the self-contradictory status of attempts to express such differences, allows some entities, namely, concepts and verbs, to have double roles in a proposition.

This 'breaking down' is far from an isolated occurrence in the *Principles*. A related case arises from Russell's view about how concepts occur in a proposition. According to Russell, the elements of a proposition provide the meaning of the proposition. These elements may include denoting concepts, both indefinite ones like *a man* and definite ones like *the last man*. Denoting concepts play the dual role of being the meaning of certain words and phrases within a sentence expressing a proposition, and also denoting something. Besides being a meaning of an expression (e.g. the meaning of 'man' is the denoting concept *man*), denoting concepts denote what falls under them (e.g. the denoting concept *man* denotes Socrates, Bismarck, etc.). In manuscripts from 1903 and 1904 Russell is preoccupied with this issue of meaning and denoting.[3] Russell wants to maintain that a logical, not a merely psychological or linguistic, connection exists between the denoting concept as a meaning and as denoting. In his 1905 paper 'On Denoting' he points out that when we attempt to talk about the concept as a meaning, as in the 'the meaning of "man"', we make the concept into the subject term in a proposition, and then what we express is not what we intend to express. He writes:

> When we wish to speak about the *meaning* of a denoting phrase, as opposed to its denotation, the natural mode of doing so is by inverted commas . . . We say, to begin with, that when C occurs it is the *denotation* that we are speaking about; but when 'C' occurs, it is the *meaning*. Now the relation of meaning to denotation is not merely linguistic through the phrase: there must be a logical relation involved, which we express by saying that the meaning denotes the denotation. But the difficulty which confronts us is that we cannot succeed in *both* preserving the connexion of meaning and denotation *and* preventing them from being one and the same; also that the meaning cannot be got at except by means of denoting phrases.[4]

Russell's solution to the problem of phrases that have meaning without denoting is given in the 1905 paper 'On Denoting' in his theory of descriptions. Russell's analysis converts what appear to be expressions denoting entities into propositions in which no such expressions appear. On his analysis, denoting phrases like 'The present King of France' and 'a man' are shown to be equivalent to more complicated expressions. For example, the definite description 'the present King of France' is analysed as $\exists x[Kx \,\&\, \forall y (Ky \rightarrow y = x)]$, 'there is only one present King of France'. The indefinite 'a man' in 'there is a man' is analysed by $\exists x Mx$. The analysis of expressions for denoting concepts reduces them to propositions containing propositional functions and quantifiers like 'something' and 'everything'.

This theory of definite and indefinite descriptions makes it possible to resolve the meaning/denotation problems presented by Russell's theory of denoting concepts precisely by showing that there need be no denoting concepts such as *the man* and *a man*, and hence no problem with their dual role. Russell's technique covers a host of different sorts of cases. Thus Russell shows that the truth of certain assertions (truths about classes, bodies, minds, etc.) can be maintained even though certain phrases in them that apparently denote entities are broken up and expanded. Thus the original phrases are shown to be dependent on being expanded into propositions; that is, they are 'incomplete symbols'. As Russell writes in the *Principia*:

> Whenever the grammatical subject of a proposition can be supposed not to exist without rendering the proposition meaningless, it is plain that the grammatical subject is not a proper name . . . Thus in all such cases, the proposition must be capable of being so analysed that what was the grammatical subject shall have disappeared.[5]

By showing that there need be no denoting concepts such as *the man* and *a man*, and hence no problem with their dual role, the theory of definite and indefinite descriptions makes it possible to resolve the meaning/denotation problems presented by Russell's theory of denoting concepts. The theory of incomplete symbols allows Russell to withdraw commitment to some of the entities in his rich ontology; thus he subsequently shows that the truth of assertions about classes, bodies, minds, and so on can be maintained even though certain phrases in these assertions are broken up and expanded in such a way that they no longer denote a single entity.

Sentences or phrases ('Caesar died', 'the death of Caesar') seem to imply the existence of a corresponding single object, the-death-of-Caesar, but from the standpoint described above, such sentences and sentence-phrases are merely incomplete symbols, meaningless phrases, which, like all other cases of incomplete symbols, require supplementation in order to express a meaning. Since it is only in the act of judging (doubting, wishing, etc.) that makes such phrases acquire a complete meaning, the propositions they purport to denote do not exist as such, but emerge only in the acts of cognition through which these phrases are broken up and acquire meaning.[6] As Russell repeatedly says, we can therefore talk about propositions for the purposes of logic, while acknowledging that there are no such single entities.

In its mature form, Russell's multiple relation theory of judgement gives an account of the cognition through which the fragmentary meanings of incomplete phrases come to express propositions. In 1904 he writes that, 'the question as to the nature of propositions is distinct from all questions of knowledge'; by 1906 and officially by 1910 Russell no longer believes this to be true.[7] By eliminating propositions as entities and conceiving of them as mere words or incomplete symbols Russell removes propositions from the domain of logic, and, by turning to a theory of judging to provide the context in which the phrases purporting to denote propositions make sense, he relocates the study of propositions within a theory of mind and knowledge, for it is these disciplines that he thinks contain an answer to how symbols have meaning.

The Impact of Meinong on Russell's Response to the Liar Paradox

The multiple relation theory of judgement replaces a doctrine of propositions as complex entities and it therefore appears to take their place only when such purported entities are, for various reasons and in various ways, being eliminated. But why are they?

Though tensions exist in Russell's notion of an objective proposition, they are not the sole or even the most pressing reason behind his decision to make do without propositions. Moreover, though the techniques developed in his 1905 paper 'On Denoting' permit him to eliminate propositions, they are not the only techniques he uses, and his experiments with different ways of getting along without propositions are bound up with an evolution in his view of the nature of belief as a cognitive act or state. The issue of his motivation to dispose of propositions and the issue of his experimentation with ways of using belief to eliminate propositions are interwoven with his shifting view of belief itself, and together these strands form a very complex story. Briefly, Russell's motivation to eliminate propositions – initially, just some kinds of propositions – springs from his need to protect his system of logic, in which propositions play a role, from various paradoxes affecting propositions. At the same time, his new fascination with and embrace of Alexius Meinong's descriptive psychology brings questions concerning the nature of cognition to the foreground, so that when Russell employs states of belief and disbelief in various ways to replace propositions, his impetus is partly due to his new excitement about a field he had for the most part ignored. These developments take place in the period between 1904 and 1906 and require further explanation. The story of that part of the development involves two separate issues: Russell's embrace of Meinong and his struggles to overcome paradoxes of propositions.

Meinong broadens Russell's conception of what is philosophically respectable work to include psychological questions about the nature and content of the mind. Such an investigation is exemplified in Russell's 1904 paper 'Meinong's Theory of Complexes and Assumptions', in which Russell enthusiastically reviews Meinong's doctrines and classification of various types of mental relations – such as belief, supposition, and assumption – as well as his largely descriptive approach. In the *Principles* the notions of mind and consciousness are not themselves subjects of explicit, extended study; the mind is assumed to be passive and receptive in acquaintance and the notion of direct perception serves principally the negative function of helping to articulate Russell's rejection of the Idealist doctrine that the structure of mind determines or constitutes what things are. Once he begins to ask questions about the mind and to do so from the perspective of classifying experiences whose conditions are psychological in nature, the concepts employed but unexamined in the *Principles* subtly shift. For example, the distinction between knowing a thing directly and knowledge about the thing appears in the *Principles* as well as in some of Russell's unpublished manuscript notes from 1904–05; indeed the term 'acquaintance' is used in connection with the principle that we must have direct acquaintance with meanings in a manuscript from 1903.[8] But, as we shall see later, when Russell uses the phrase 'knowledge by acquaintance' in 1913, it is not the same notion of knowing a thing directly presented in the *Principles of Mathematics*.

Meinong's work also contributes certain ideas to Russell's philosophical lexicon. In particular, he adopts Meinong's conception of belief as a single state of mind synonymous with an idea or thought, and begins to ask questions such as whether in acts of affirming p and assuming p the mind relates to the same or different objective propositions.[9] He is not wholly in agreement with Meinong. For example, since no such entities are ever presented to the mind Meinong denies the existence of negative objective propositions and reduces disbelief in not p to belief in p. Anticipating an argument he uses in 1918 in defence of negative facts, Russell rejects the attempt to replace negative propositions with disbelief in positive ones on the grounds that it fails to explain what it is that we know when our belief that not-p is true. If we believe not-p and the belief is true, then we know something, and since knowledge must be objective and not merely express disbelief, a negative proposition must underlie the truth of a belief that not p. Anticipating a further theme in his defence of negative facts, Russell claims that negative propositions exist even though we perceive only affirmative ones; 'there is', he says, 'no validity in Meinong's argument that the presentations must be perceptible'.[10] He writes: 'direct inspection, I think, will show that the state of mind in which we reject a proposition is not the same as that in which we accept its negation. Again the Law of Excluded Middle may be stated in the form: if p is denied, not-p must be asserted; its form, it is true, is too psychological to be ultimate, but the point is, that it is still significant and not a tautology.'[11] The notion of belief and the reduction of negative propositions to states of disbelief reappear, however, in Russell's own notes, as he attempts various methods of eliminating paradoxes of propositions.

In the *Principles* and later texts, a propositional function is a logical indefinable. Propositional functions are expressions such as 'x is a man' that stand for any one proposition from a class of propositions and become propositions by replacing the 'x' with a name (e.g. 'Socrates') and thereby giving a value (things, such as Socrates) to the argument-place indicated by 'x'.[12] As Russell discovers early on, paradoxes result when certain *prima facie* innocuous propositional functions (or propositions) are allowed to take certain values – such as themselves, in the classic instance.[13] The discovery that paradoxes arise from apparently innocuous concepts and assumptions forces Russell, in the *Principles* and in many papers in years following that work, to attempt to curb the contradictions. He does so in two related moves. One is to show that certain purported entities (such as classes) are incomplete symbols. As non-entities and hence not potential arguments to a propositional function, he eliminates contexts (such as the class of all classes not members of themselves) that lead to paradoxes. Another move is to place restrictions on the range of significance of a propositional function; that is, to restrict the values (things, propositional functions, functions of propositional functions, etc.) which will yield a significant proposition. This general approach, developed over a decade, is the theory of types, coupled with the theory of incomplete symbols.

For my purposes, what is important is not Russell's mature theory of types but the way he invokes belief in the period between 1903 and 1908 as he is on his way towards the mature theory.[14] Most of Russell's work between 1903 and 1908 consists of a variety of attempts to offset logical paradoxes afflicting classes, functions, relations and propositions while addressing other, epistemological forms of paradox. An example of the latter type is the Liar or Epimenides' paradox 'every sentence I assert is false'. My focus is solely on how the notion of belief is used as Russell attempts to eliminate some, or all, kinds of propositions in his work between 1904 and 1906. Most of this work occurs in unpublished notes and papers; the most relevant manuscripts for my purposes are 'Paradox of the Liar' (September 1906) and 'Types' (first half of 1907).[15] In these papers he encounters the problem of the content of false belief, resorts to a multiple relation theory of belief that employs ideas, and treats the view of belief as a single thing as open to paradox; these difficulties, I believe, constitute the motivation for the elimination of propositions and the adoption of the multiple relation theory of belief. As the theory emerges, it uses and reshapes the concept of belief Russell absorbs from Meinong.

It is Russell's elimination of the concept *falsity* that first brings Meinong's notion of belief into play. In 'Paradox of the Liar' Russell considers propositions about propositions, specifically those that deny a proposition or that assert that a proposition is false. By eliminating the possibility of propositions of the form '*p* is false' and 'not-*p*' he will avoid the Liar paradox, he thinks, as it will then be impossible to refer to all of one's lies, that is, to all of one's false propositions. He can eliminate them, furthermore, by reducing propositions about the falsity of propositions to states of disbelief towards propositions. He writes:

> Statements involving 'not' express disbelief in *p*, i.e. an objective *p* is never negative and negation is psychological. Also, to say '*x* is false' is to express disbelief in *x*.[16]

Russell therefore accepts what he earlier held against Meinong, namely that there is only one objective proposition, which may be asserted or denied, and 'there is no such object as "not-*p*" or "*p* is false"'.[17] Since he has already raised objections to this view in his reviews of Meinong,[18] it's no surprise that he immediately notes difficulties.[19] First, we must strain to apply the account to molecular propositions like 'not-*p* or *q*' as there is no obvious sense in which the whole or its constituents are either believed or disbelieved. Second, if both *p* and *q* are false and thus non-entities it is a mystery what constitutes the truth of conditionals 'if *p* then *q*' with a false antecedent and a false consequent. Russell's elimination of false propositions by means of reducing falsehood to disbelief is a strand distinct from but at times (as in 1913) joined to his use of belief as the supplement or context giving meaning to sentences as incomplete symbols.

This is not the only strand that feeds into his mature multiple relation theory of belief. In 'Types' Russell considers eliminating false propositions by introducing the truth of a belief in a false proposition. 'We don't', he says, 'have to interpret fx when fx is false, but only "A believes fx" when this is true but fx is false.'[20] But his analysis goes further and reduces both true and false propositions to a complex of ideas constituting a person's belief. As the second sentence below shows, he is momentarily willing to deny that in belief the relevant objects are objects known by acquaintance:

> Take 'A believes $\phi(x,y)$'. We shall say that $\phi(x,y)$ is not itself before A's mind at all; but that if we call i'x, i'y the ideas of x and y, i'x and i'y are in A's mind, and here there [is] a relation analogous to ϕ, which we may call ϕ_i. Thus 'belief in $\phi(x,y)$ exists' is 'f_1(i'x, i'y)', i.e. 'the ideas of x and y are in fact related in the way (ϕ_i) corresponding to the relation f between x and y'. In this way we can explain belief in false prop[osition]s without supposing that there are any prop[osition]s.[21]

At the same time he uses belief as a complex of ideas to eliminate propositions, Russell begins to address the difficulties posed by belief as a single entity. The question also occurs in his 1906 'On the Nature of Truth and Falsehood', and Russell there denies that belief is a single thing or a state of mind,[22] pointing to 'On Denoting', written a few months prior, as the source of the techniques enabling him to show that belief is not a single thing. He writes:

> [A] belief, if this view is adopted, will not consist of one idea with a complex object, but will consist of several related ideas . . . A *belief* will then differ from an idea or presentation by the fact that it will consist of several interrelated ideas.[23]

Russell motivates the elimination of beliefs in 'On the Nature of Truth' by reference to the Liar paradox. 'There are', he says, difficulties in . . . regarding a belief [as a single state of mind]. The chief of these difficulties is derived from paradoxes analogous to that of the liar, e.g. from the man who believes that all of his beliefs are mistaken . . . We can escape this paradox if a belief cannot be validly treated as a single thing.[24]

In 'Types', however, Russell is unwilling to allow belief to be a single thing not because of the Liar paradox but because of a quite different logical paradox.

[A] belief (unless one with apparent variables) is not a single state of mind but a complex involving transitions, for if there is a belief for each proposition, then, if beliefs are individuals, there will be (at least) as many individuals as propositions, which is impossible.[25]

This analysis – of belief as a multiple relation of ideas – is joined in Russell's 1906 paper to his theory of incomplete symbols, constituting the original (or an original) form of that doctrine. In 1910 Russell republishes the 1906 paper above, extracting the portion presenting the theory of belief as a complex of ideas and replacing it with 'The Nature of Truth and Falsehood' in which he officially embraces the multiple relation theory. My present point has been to show that it and the version presented in 'Types', as well as the reduction of false belief to states of disbelief, constitute important strands in the origin of his mature theory of belief. They are rooted in what he takes from Meinong, as well as in his struggles to avoid the various kinds of contradictions to which his doctrine of objective propositions is prone.

These early notes show, furthermore, that from the beginning in Russell's shift towards the multiple relation theory he confronts the problem of the content of belief, especially of false beliefs. This is apparent when we consider Russell's early attempts to analyse belief, not as a complex of ideas, but as a complex of things. In 'Paradox of the Liar' Russell replaces a doctrine of objective true and false propositions with a theory of belief as a relation among objects, regarding belief in a proposition not as 'a thought related to a proposition, but as a thought related to the constituents of the proposition'.[26] On this theory false beliefs have meaning by virtue of a thought being related 'to several objects in a different way from that in which a right belief about those objects would be related to them'.[27] The trouble is that nothing corresponds to the belief if in a false belief a thought is related to entities in a false way; or, as Russell puts it in 'Types', the doctrine amounts to 'the old, old theory that the man who believes what is false believes nothing'.[28] Of course on this view true beliefs are also, in a sense, beliefs in 'nothing' or in no single thing, but at least there are related entities to provide meaning; in the case of false belief no relation of entities exists and no analysis into related entities is possible:

> The difference is that, in the case of true props, the analysis into related entities seems plausible; but in the case of false props it seems implausible.[29]

This worry gets little or no direct attention when Russell adopts his mature theory of belief as constituted by objects. As we shall see, his theory remains vulnerable on precisely this point, and problems of content form a significant theme in the *Theory of Knowledge*. Why, then, did the problem fade into the background? One reason why this may have faded from view emerges from consideration of Russell's shifting theory of truth.

Problems for an Account of Truth

It has become commonplace to say that Russell's theory of truth provides the motivation for his introducing the multiple relation theory. Ramsey appears to be the first to attribute this motivation to Russell's development of the theory of knowledge; his 1927 discussion of analysis of judgement describes Russell's shift to the multiple relation theory as moving away from a simple explanation of the objective factor in belief (truth or false are un-analysable properties) due to 'incredulity of the existence of such objects' and 'the mysterious nature of the difference . . . between truth and falsehood'.[30] To understand his point we have to turn back to Russell's doctrine of objective propositions.

If propositions are objective complexes whose constituents – concepts and particulars – are bound by an external relation, then the difference between a proposition when it is true and the same proposition when it is false must be a difference in their relation to the concept *truth*. Similarly, the one and the same entity that occurs as a verbal subject (e.g. 'the death of Caesar') and as the verb in a proposition ('Caesar died') differs in these cases in its relation to truth. But describing the difference is problematic. The difference can't be explained as a difference in internal relation to the concept *truth* or the two occurrences would be different entities, but it can't be explained in terms of their external relation to *truth*, since a false proposition does not become true (or a logical subject become a proposition) by adding the concept *true*.[31] It isn't enough to say that the difference is only psychological, and Russell concludes that being true (or being a proposition) is a non-analysable quality.[32] We cannot talk about what is distinctive about the verb when it occurs as an assertion; what is unique to assertion is lost in analysis. In 1904 Russell notes that as a consequence of his theory that nothing can be said about truth and falsity except that they are distinct, the difference between being true and being false amounts to an empty distinction:

> It may be said . . . that some propositions are true and some are false, just as some roses are red and some white; . . . But this seems to leave our preference for truth a mere unaccountable prejudice, and in no way to answer to the feeling of truth and falsehood.[33]

When he adopts his multiple relation theory, Russell gives as a point in its favour that it allows him to explain the nature of truth and falsehood.[34] Comments like these seem to suggest that inadequacies in his theory of truth lie behind Russell's elimination of objective propositions in favour of the multiple relation theory of judgement. Nevertheless, I do not believe this to be the case.

First, the text from which the passage above is taken actually comes out in favour of Russell's doctrine of truth, since the alternative, explaining the truth of a proposition in terms of a correspondence with fact, is a tautology. It is a tautology, that is, because in this period Russell embraces objective propositions, and for him 'a fact appears to be merely a true proposition'.[35] Thus in 'On the Nature of Truth and Falsehood', Russell argues that in using the notion of *correspondence* to define the notion of *truth* we have to use *truth* to define *correspondence,* and the doctrine of correspondence is therefore, at bottom, empty.[36] For these reasons, Russell adheres to his view of propositions despite the limits on explaining truth until other pressures, described above, persuade him to relinquish it and new techniques give him the means to do so.

Second, Russell can hardly have been motivated to adopt the new theory of judgement because of its superior doctrine of truth, since in fact he initially rejects it (as a relation among ideas) on the grounds that it involves what he sees as a problematic correspondence theory of truth. This becomes clear if we return to his introduction of the multiple relation theory in 1906 as an analysis of a single state of belief into a complex of ideas. On that doctrine the belief aRb consists of a relation between the idea of a, the idea of b and the idea of their relation R. Since the fact supposed to correspond to the belief is less complex, consisting only of a's relation to b, the correspondence seems to break down.[37] As Russell puts it:

> There is great difficulty in explaining what this correspondence consists of, since for example, the belief that A and B have the relation R must be a *three-*termed relation of the ideas of A and B and R. Whether a satisfactory definition of the correspondence is possible, I do not know.[38]

On Russell's 1910 doctrine, judgement is a multiple relation among objects and therefore avoids the problems of correspondence faced by the 1906 version. It also avoids the difficulties he sees in a pragmatist account: in between the publication of this paper in 1906 and Russell's official embrace of the multiple relation theory in 1910, his attention is drawn to the pragmatist account of truth, and his conception of what is desirable in a theory of truth develops in part as a rejection of their account, which he says identifies truth with what furthers our purposes,[39] fails to explain how truth is based on fact and differs from falsity,[40] and gives a criterion by which we judge truth rather than the meaning of the word 'true'. Thus when his 1910 theory of judgement is promoted as addressing what we mean by 'true' and not just a criterion, and as explaining the *nature* of true and false – what true or false *is* – Russell is speaking simultaneously to pragmatism and to his own earlier doctrines. Though Russell elaborates on the virtues of the 1910 doctrine of judgement – it does justice to the role of the judge and the role of the facts[41] – these qualities are consequences of a theory adopted for other reasons and not reasons for its adoption.

Acquaintance and Belief

Russell admits in the 1906 paper that his theory is 'very likely open to fatal objections' and abandons the theory of belief as a relation holding among ideas.[42] The multiple relation theory he officially adopts in 1910 explains judgement or belief as a many-placed relation holding between a subject and the objects and relation constituting its belief, and in *Theory of Knowledge*, the number of terms (objects, relation and subject) related by belief determines where these complexes fall within a hierarchy.[43] Though the fatal problems of correspondence are avoided in 1910 by viewing objects rather than ideas as related by belief into a fact, Russell has other reasons for insisting that belief be composed of things and not ideas. This view of belief is not an obvious one. It might be thought that when we believe our belief consists of the ideas or thoughts corresponding to the various objects. For example, if I believe that mercury is heavier than gold, my belief, it might seem, adjoins an idea of *mercury* to the idea of *gold*. Truth and error could then be defined as the correspondence or lack of correspondence of my complex of ideas to some actual state of affairs, the relative weight of mercury and gold. Russell's reasons for rejecting this view bear in part on his conception of knowledge and the role acquaintance and descriptions play in that conception. First, in judging we normally attempt to convey information about the world. For example, in believing that mercury is heavier than gold, we are neither attributing extramental properties like *heavier* to an idea nor are we attributing the idea of *heavier* to an idea of *gold*. Rather, as he says in *Theory of Knowledge*, 'my judging obviously consists in my believing that there is a relation between actual objects, *mercury* and *gold*'.[44]

Second, in order to judge at all we have to know what we are judging, and on Russell's atomistic doctrine of meaning, we do so by having acquaintance with the objects (the meanings) corresponding to the words used to express the judgement. An important aspect of Russell's requirement that we know what we are judging is that what we grasp cannot be such as to leave open the possibility of our being in error: the existence of the objects grasped must be indubitable data of direct experience.[45] Ordinary objects cannot give this guarantee, and Russell treats purported names for such objects as disguised descriptions whose meaning is ultimately derived from one's acquaintance with other, indubitable data. All of the terms in a description, including (until 1913) any personal reference to self must, ultimately, be cashed out in terms of something the judge has directly experienced, by means of the techniques of the theory of descriptions. Thus in believing we are acquainted with objects, though the things meant, believed in and constitutive of a belief fact are not the naïve objects of common sense – in the 1910–1912 period Russell is agnostic on the question of their existence – but sense data and universals.

Since Russell's point is to elaborate the different ways of being conscious of objects, and none of the ways of being conscious – of being acquainted – is more typical than others, the category *acquaintance* is more inclusive than the above remarks suggest. Russell applies the term 'acquaintance' to external perception – seeing, hearing, touching, etc. – of particular colours, sounds or tactile sensations, to the inner senses – imagination, hallucination, dreaming and introspection – and to our grasp of universals.[46] But unlike objects that continue to affect the world in our absence, objects in his sense are independent of the initiating event or occasion on which we first apprehend them. Thus we can be acquainted with data that began to exist for us in the (immediate) past, such as when we continue to hear the chimes of a bell after the motion of the bell and the sound waves have ceased,[47] and we can acquire acquaintance with a recondite datum as the end result of other acts of acquaintance, as in grasping a universal on the basis of particular experiences through a difficult process of analysis.[48]

Moreover, Russell views the complexity or simplicity of what we perceive as a function of our act of perception, invoking a cognitive relation called 'attention' as the means by which we adjust our sights to see a datum as complex or as simple. The mind, which is receptive but not inert, can, depending on its attention, apprehend a particular colour-datum, for example, as a field of colours and shapes or as a unit. (Indeed, attention is connected to the notion of degrees of difficulty and abstractness since acquaintance involves no special exertion, while attention does.) This aspect of consciousness underlies the possibility of a transition from dual relations such as acquaintance to multiple relations that are self-evident.

Judgements of Perception

The ability of consciousness to shift from perception of a simple to perception of a complex seen *as* complex underlies Russell's account of the link between perception and self-evident judgements. Since we can alternate between seeing things as simple and seeing them as complex, we may shift from perceiving a complex (such as a-before-b) to judging that it is a complex, and when we do so, we segue from a dual relation, which is indubitable, to a multiple relation of judging that, at least ideally, is self-evident. In *Principia*, Russell writes:

> The complex object 'a-in-the-relation-R-to-b' may be capable of being *perceived*; when perceived, it is perceived as one object. Attention may show that it is complex; we then *judge* that a and b stand in the relation R. Such a judgement, being derived from perception by mere attention, may be called a 'judgement of perception'.[49]

Russell intends his notion of a judgement of perception to give a theoretical account of the nature of the truth of judgement, not an account of our actual process of judging. Since such a judgement is by definition derived from direct perception of a complex object of acquaintance, and since 'an object of acquaintance cannot be nothing', it follows that judgements of perception are those that 'must be true'.[50] Granted, it is possible to think we have a judgement of perception when we have only a false belief. This is because in order to arrive at a judgement of perception we have to analyse a perception and the analysis can go wrong: we can be mistaken despite the reality on which such judgements are based. In *Principia* we read:

> [T]his does not mean that, in a judgement which appears to us to be one of perception, we are sure of not being in error, since we may err in thinking that our judgement has really been derived merely by analysis of what has been perceived.[51]

In *Problems of Philosophy* he gives an example:

> Suppose we first perceive the sun shining, which is a complex fact, and thence proceed to make the judgement 'the sun is shining'. In passing from the perception to the judgement, it is necessary to analyse the given complex fact; we have to separate out 'the sun' and 'shining' as constituents of the fact. In this process it is possible to commit an error; hence even where a fact has the first or absolute kind of self-evidence, a judgement believed to correspond to the fact is not absolutely infallible, because it may not really correspond to the fact.[52]

In the *Theory of Knowledge* Russell makes a similar point when he acknowledges that we may forget or misremember the meanings of our words in the transition from perception to judgement about the perception.[53] But if his doctrine seems especially vulnerable to scepticism, that is because we have in mind the practical impossibility of making sure that our judgements of perception are correctly derived from perception, whereas his interest lies in defining self-evident truth, and this is explicated in terms of judgements based directly on analysis of an object of perception.

Types in *Principia*

In the *Principia*, judgements – or propositions, to speak in incomplete symbols – divide into types. The central idea in Russell's type theory is his 'vicious circle' thesis; namely, that a propositional function is *meaningful* only if its values, propositions, are a well-defined totality.[54] That is, a propositional function presupposes some class of propositions (more properly, of judgements) as values *of* a propositional function.[55] Thus, 'the values of a function are presupposed by the function, not vice versa'.[56] The vicious circle doctrine blocks paradoxes by disallowing propositional functions to be asserted of themselves – which, could it occur, would result in an expanding totality of propositions (values of the propositional function) that is not well defined. The kind of propositional value (i.e. the kind of judgement made) fixes the order of the propositional function as one that denotes values (propositions) of that kind. That is, the doctrine stratifies propositional functions into a hierarchy: there are elementary propositional functions in which no apparent variables occur, and whose values are all elementary judgements, and so forth. But propositions are tied to propositional functions; that is, propositions result when we replace the variables in a propositional function with names. What results must assert a definite (true or false) proposition. To assert a definite proposition, the names which replace the variables in a propositional function can't be of any kind whatsoever, but have to be restricted to a certain set of arguments (e.g. men, not colours) for which the propositional function (e.g. 'x is human') in question yields a proposition which makes sense. These values *for* a propositional function define the range of significance – the 'type' – of the propositional function.

The different kinds of judgements are explained in epistemological terms. For example, to assert that a certain property belongs to an object (or a relation obtains between objects) is, according to Russell, to make an elementary judgement.[57] Acts of elementary judgement require no other knowledge than the complex that would have to exist if the judgement is true. What could verify the judgement 'Fa' is perception of the complex F-a. An assertion of 'Fa' is true if the complex F-a exists, and false otherwise.[58] 'Fa' has a *kind* of truth; in fact, the most basic kind. The truth of different kinds of judgements seems to presuppose the link between perception of complexes and judgements of perception. Though his discussion of the connection between judgements of perception and elementary judgements is sketchy at best, Russell may mean to define the truth of elementary judgements, which are not derived from analysis of a present experience, in terms of the self-evidence they would by definition possess considered as judgements of perception occurring in the presence of such an object of acquaintance. If so, the truth of elementary judgements is secured by the link between indubitable perception and judgements of perception. In any event, it is clear that the notion of truth for elementary judgements, i.e. elementary or first-order truth, defines truth for other very different kinds of judgements. For example, what makes a general judgement like 'all humans are mortal' a 'radically' new kind[59] is that more than one complex (e.g. to Socrates-is-mortal, Plato-is-mortal, etc.) corresponds to it. Yet to assert that a general judgement is true is simply to say, 'all instances of elementary judgements have elementary truth', that is, the meaning of 'true' and 'false' for general propositions is based on the meaning of these concepts for elementary ones. The notions of 'true' and 'false' arrange themselves in a hierarchy; they are systematically ambiguous, with 'different meanings, appropriate to propositions of different kinds'.[60]

Judging and the Sense of a Relation

Let me now turn from the details of the emerging multiple relation theory of judgement so as to lay out some of the problems it poses in the 1910–1912 period in which Russell fully embraces it. On the multiple relation theory items occur singly in a multiple arrangement. How, then, is belief able to discriminate between the belief whose sense (or direction) is that the pen is to the left of the cup and the belief whose sense (or direction) is that the cup is to the left of the pen? But what relation, occurring in the judgement fact, is responsible for discriminating between different senses? Is it the super-ordinate relation *judging* or the subordinate relation (e.g. *loves*)? In 1910 *sense* appears to be a function of so-called subordinate relations such as *loves*. In the 1910 paper 'On the Nature of Truth and Falsehood', Russell claims that:

> The relation must not be abstractly before the mind, but must be before it as proceeding from a to b rather than from b to a . . . We may distinguish two 'senses' of a relation, according as it goes from a to b or from b to a. Then the relation as it enters into the judgement must have a 'sense', and in the corresponding complex it must have the same sense. Thus the judgement that two terms have a certain relation R is the relation of the mind to the two terms and the relation R with the appropriate sense: the corresponding complex consists of the two terms related by the relation R with the same sense. The judgement is true when there is such a complex, and false when there is not.[61]

In 1911, G. F. Stout objects that the relation is supposed to occur as an object of acquaintance or term but that if it occurs with a sense it does more.[62] Russell concedes the point, saying:

> As regards the sense of the relation r in judging ArB, you make a point which had already occurred to me . . . [I]n the act of judging that ArB, the sense must be confined to judging, and must not appear in the r. But judging being a multiple relation, its sense is not merely twofold like that of a dual relation, and the judging alone may arrange the terms in the order Mind, A, r, B, as opposed to Mind, B, r, A.[63]

As a result, Russell restates the theory in 1912 so that 'the relation of judging puts things in order' and differences of sense are built into the super-ordinate relation *judging*.[64] This theory makes it difficult to explain how false judgements are possible, since a judgement is true when the relation it asserts holds, and judging is here given the task of uniting the items. The theory is vulnerable to the accusation that it makes the sense of a judgement too subjective as well as making it impossible to explain how a judgement can be false.

We have been looking at the difference between judging that a is greater than b and judging that b is greater than a. This is not the only dimension of sense Russell acknowledges. In the 1903 *Principles*[65] he also distinguishes between judging that a is greater than b and judging that b is less than a; judgements asserting these cases correspond to different complexes,[66] and this species of difference is also called a 'difference of sense'.[67] Where others might be tempted to admit difference of sense in the first case but not the second, for Russell the difference in both cases has the same status. It is neither merely psychological nor merely linguistic. Russell retains this view of sense in 1910–1912 even though he has eliminated objective propositions. His multiple relation theory of belief therefore has to account for both kinds of differences of sense in exactly the same way. If Russell feels the need to distinguish sense in this more subtle fashion in 1910 and 1912, he doesn't say so, and it isn't clear how he could, given the resources of his theory. In the *Theory of Knowledge* he rejects the ontological suggestions of such a distinction, viewing judgements that a is less than b as only a transcriptional variant of the judgement that b is greater than a. He also denies that relations can have sense and that judging can confer sense.

Difficulties

In the present section, I canvas some (not all) difficulties that arise within Russell's doctrines of belief and perception. Many of these difficulties overlap with issues raised directly or indirectly in the *Theory of Knowledge.*

A single judgement is said to be composed of the objects it collects together – that is, in being judged, it comprises a relational fact composed of the mind, a judging relation and the other terms, among them a relation. One difficulty for the multiple relation theory (in both the 1910 and 1912 versions) emerges if we focus on it as a way of knowing complexes. Unlike perception, belief is not a direct relation to a complex, that is, the complex is not a single object of acquaintance such as, e.g., this white patch before me. And unlike a judgement of perception, there need be no present complex unity involved in the judgement. As mentioned, the multiple relation theory of truth relies on constituents occurring as separate items of acquaintance and is not tied to acquaintance with the unity of those constituents. The constituents can therefore fail to be united.

But if there is no perception of a unity or arrangement of these items (e.g. *loves*, Desdemona and Cassio), *where* are they arranged? Where is the relating supposed to occur? The items comprising a belief are objects, not ideas, and if they are believed to form a complex, either the complex must already exist, or it is made to exist by our believing in it, or what we are believing engages the items otherwise than as occurring in a complex. None of these alternatives is acceptable to Russell, so the problem remains: how is he to give meaning to the notion that someone believes certain items to be related but they need not in fact be related? In 1913 Russell will attempt to provide this by means of bringing in a non-mental, non-physical medium of form.[68] Belief unifies items occurring in a complex by referring them to and thinking of them through an abstract domain of form.

In addition, the multiple relation theory makes it impossible to define what is common to different expressions of the same 'propositional content'. Whatever account of belief-events we give, it must be possible to explain how there is a common core meaning to my belief that gold is heavy and your belief that *heaviness* is a property of gold. How does Russell's multiple relation theory explain the proposition? That is, how does it account for what is common to different acts and expressions of believing? Russell's theory of belief relies on the actual occurrence of the belief, which is to say the actual particulars involved. These particulars will differ in different cases of belief, and therefore will yield more distinctions of meaning than would seem to be desirable in a theory of belief. In order to distinguish two acts of belief which otherwise have the same content, Russell asserts that a belief is individuated by something unique, the peculiarly mental element, or self. But then it becomes puzzling how there can be any common proposition or meaning to different occurring beliefs. If being uniquely tied to an act or knowing subject provides a belief with its meaning, *that* meaning cannot also be universal, the same belief grasped or believed by other believers. These two problems are connected: If there is no perception of a unity, where is the relating supposed to occur? For if the universals contained in the belief are linked to a particular person's belief, then it would seem that the particular way the person expresses that belief linguistically (e.g. 'Brutus stabbed and killed Caesar') is the important thing. But then we seem not to be able to identify the belief with that which is expressed by sentences we might want to say mean the same thing (e.g. 'Caesar was stabbed and killed by Brutus').

And what is the status of the items – especially the relation – in belief? On Russell's analysis, the subordinate relation (e.g. *loves*) that occurs in a belief occurs as a term able to be named. Similarly, *judging* itself is a term of the belief-fact. But taken as individuals, all the terms enter into the fact the same way and there is no reason to differentiate between entities.

Another set of difficulties arises from Russell's notion of perception. This notion is obscure in several respects. Russell does not clearly distinguish perception and sensation. Sensation, one might think, is presupposed by perception but not identical with it, since the same sensation can yield different perceptions. The cube seen in different ways is a classic example of this. If Russell's notion of acquaintance means perception, this is a problem for him because acquaintance is intended to be the bedrock of certain knowledge. But perhaps acquaintance is more like pure sensation. Against this stands the fact that Russell allows particular sense data to be seen *as* complex, and presumably brute sensation is incompatible with seeing something *as* complex. For seeing something as complex is a 'seeing' that presupposes a way of categorizing experience.

This last point raises additional problems. To hold that we perceive a complex seems to bring in or presuppose some kind of judgement, which is on Russell's view a multiple relation. But presumably Russell wishes to distinguish perception from belief. Russell's notion of attention, which he uses to explain the transition between acquaintance and judgements of immediate acquaintance, shares this problem. Attention cannot be merely a kind of acquaintance – for then how we proceed from it to judgement is unclear –

or a multiple relation, for then the transition to judgement has been presupposed. In general, Russell does not explain the notion of a transition from simple perception to complex perception: what is it to perceive a complex except to see *that* constituents are combined in such and such a way? That is, if a-before-b is perceived it arguably already involves something like a propositional form.

But if to perceive a complex is to see that constituents are combined in such and such a way then perhaps there are other ways of being combined, using the same data. To concede that the data do not arrange themselves in any single pattern for us is to concede that the notion of a *fact* detaches from the doctrine that elements and structure completely determine the different facts to be judged. Such a view not only is in tension with Russell's core analysis of meaning and acquaintance, it is also in tension with Russell's notion of a simple, at least in the predominating sense in which Russell uses this notion. If we acknowledge that facts involve the way the data are seen – and that the way they are seen is not some constituent or structural property – then it becomes difficult to support the notion of a passive mind receiving a presentation of a pure, unadulterated datum.

As Pears has noted, there is an unbridgeable gap between attending to the complex as an object named by a proper name, and arriving at a judgement, which is a dual relation. If we attend to the complex as an object referred to by a proper name, then to use this name is to use a vacuous term, i.e. not to make a substantive judgement.[69] For to use names in a way in which they are informative and can be said to amount to judging is to require some other kind of information than anything given in mere perception of the complex itself. After all, perception or acquaintance is supposed to differ from judgement precisely in being uninformative. In order to judge a complex we have to already understand its analysis: which items are relations and which ones are terms. This information is not conveyed by perception of the complex itself, however. Finally, it is unclear how the certainty of the meaning conveyed by acquaintance can transfer over to the complex judgement – how one and the same item can be known to be the simple that is subsequently seen as complex – unless there is some accompanying knowledge in the grasp of it *as* a simple, that is, some standpoint from which to compare it with the same thing seen as complex.

Wittgenstein, Form and the Problem of Complexes

Differences in sense arise despite the fact that complexes have the same ingredients in the same form. The notion of form, which is highlighted by the problem of sense, receives Russell's attention, however, in connection to another problem, that of non-existent complexes. Some of Russell's first comments concerning work he wishes to leave to Wittgenstein concern form. By the autumn of 1912 Russell's respect for Wittgenstein has grown to the point that he imagines the younger man to be his intellectual successor, and on several occasions, writing to Ottoline, he expresses a wish to leave certain difficulties to Wittgenstein. One of the issues he wants to hand over to Wittgenstein concerns the nature of form, or rather, how to define the form of a complex such that it applies to non-existent complexes as well as existing ones. Russell explicitly raises this issue in a short manuscript called 'What is Logic?' written in September and October of 1912.[70] The notes concentrate on the nature of propositions and forms, while working within a broad conception of logic as the study of forms. Propositions must be true or false, but there are no objective false propositions, that is, propositions, true or false, exist only as words, incomplete symbols, rather than as complexes. In 1904 he thought the nature of proposition was a logical question and 'distinct from all questions of knowledge', but by 1910 he officially removed propositions from the concern of logic and located it in the theory of knowledge. Here he reiterates that point: logic is therefore 'not concerned with propositions' but with complexes. Moreover, logic is concerned with the forms of complexes, as the form of a complex is not a mere symbol but something objective, something in common to all complexes of that form. (On pain of starting an endless regress it can't be a genuine constituent of the complex.)[71]

The notion of the form of a complex is linked with the concept of substituting certain entities in a complex for others so as to arrive at a different complex of the same form, but there can be no such substitution when the complex doesn't exist, and Russell's notes struggle to define form or substitution in a complex in a way that accounts for non-existent complexes. He admits that the idea of substituting in a complex 'can only have a definite meaning when the result is a complex, not when it isn't'.[72] In such a case 'you can substitute in the symbol for a complex, but not in the complex'.[73] Nevertheless, form must be taken as primitive, according to Russell. Thus he considers and quickly rejects the possibility that *being of the same form* is primitive, because this view too 'rules out non-existent complexes'.[74] Russell thus fails to solve difficulties having to do with forms of non-existent complexes, conceding in a letter to Ottoline that he is 'stuck' and that the subject is 'too difficult' and that he feels 'inclined to leave it to Wittgenstein'.[75] Russell agonizes to Ottoline both in 1913 and later in 1916 that Wittgenstein's criticism had to do with foundational problems of logic, which he clearly equates with the study of forms; and in the *Theory of Knowledge* Russell comes to the conclusion, as he puts it in 1914, in his revision of Chapter 4 of *Theory of Knowledge*, 'it is impossible to assign to the theory of knowledge a province distinct from that of logic' because 'all thought whose expression involves *propositions*, must be a fact of a different logical form from any of the series: subject-predicate facts, dual relations, triple relations, etc.'.[76]

For his part, Wittgenstein seems to have gained enormous confidence from studying with Russell, and his interests, as evident in his letters to Russell, match the sort of thing Russell says he wishes to leave to Wittgenstein: the analysis of forms and the nature of the proposition. This is especially clear in a letter he writes to Russell in January of 1913. In the letter, Wittgenstein criticizes Russell's analysis of complexes and propositions for allowing substitutions that result in nonsensical combinations. His letter opens with a general statement of his idea:[77]

> . . . I have changed my views on 'atomic' complexes: I now think that Qualities, Relations (like Love), etc. are all copulae! That means I for instance analyse a subject–predicate proposition, say, 'Socrates is human' into 'Socrates' and 'Something is human' (which I think is not complex). The reason for this is a

very fundamental one: I think there cannot be different Types of things! In other words whatever can be symbolized by a simple proper name must belong to one type. And further: every theory of types must be rendered superfluous by a proper theory of symbolism.[78]

What he means is not immediately clear, but it turns on his reflection on the nature of a symbolism. His point is that the use of the symbols that go into expressing a proposition ought by themselves to guarantee that a proposition makes sense, since that is their role, that is, to yield a proposition, i.e. a vehicle with sense. The role of certain symbols is to constitute a proposition, a vehicle of sense, and they therefore stand in the way of attempts to substitute in ways that yield nonsense.

For instance if [A] I analyse the prop[osition] Socrates is Mortal into Socrates, Mortality, and $(\exists x,y)\ \varepsilon_1\ (x,y)$ I want a theory of types to tell me that 'Mortality is Socrates' is nonsensical, because if I treat 'Mortality' as a proper name (as I did) there is nothing to prevent me to make the substitution the wrong way round. *But* if [B] I analyse [it] (as I do now) into Socrates and $(\exists x)$. x is mortal or generally into x and $(\exists x)\ \phi x$* it becomes impossible to substitute the wrong way around because the two symbols are now of a different *kind* themselves.[79]

Wittgenstein is somewhat indifferent to the particular solution – the symbolism – he suggests is correct, and he concludes the letter by saying:

What I am *most* certain of is not however the correctness of my present way of analysis, but of the fact that all theory of types must be done away with by a theory of symbolism showing that what seem to be *different kinds of things* are symbolized by different kinds of symbols which *cannot* possibly be substituted in one another's places. I hope I have made this fairly clear! *Props which I formerly wrote $e_2(a,R,b)$ I now write $R(a,b)$ and analyse them into a, b and $(\exists x,y,)R(x,y)$ not complex.[80]

His letter has received a great deal of attention, in part because he analyses complexes like R(a,b) into the objects a and b and the form, and though Wittgenstein uses bound variables to symbolize a form – as in (∃x,y,)R(x,y) – and Russell uses free variables – as in xRy – Wittgenstein's letter seems to anticipate Russell's doctrine of judgement in the *Theory of Knowledge*, where forms appear as ingredients alongside objects and the subject.[81] This raises questions of provenance; specifically, did Russell originate the idea or did Wittgenstein? There are a variety of views on that question. For example, Griffin takes the initial analysis [A] in Wittgenstein's 1913 January letter to be 'the first written occurrence of Russell's final version of the multiple version of the multiple relation theory, that which involves forms',[82] but he thinks that Wittgenstein is 'referring to a theory that he'd had from Russell'[83] and since 'we already see Russell', in 1912, 'moving logical forms toward the centre of his account of logic'.[84] Sommerville suggests that Wittgenstein got the general idea of such analyses from Russell's own earlier versions of his theory of judgement, but that the idea is his own.

Griffin and Sommerville represent varying ways of reading the provenance of the notion of form in Russell's 1913 theory of judgement. I will not attempt to decide which reading is correct, nor will I attempt to survey the various other readings that have been given. In the next chapter I will, however, give a reading of the *Theory of Knowledge* and of the objections to which Russell responds in which I assume that the notion of form *is* new to Russell's explicit analysis of judgement but is also already an ingredient in his nascent account of our understanding of judgements. Right now my point is to show that Russell and Wittgenstein are both aware and working on issues concerning substitution, the forms of atomic complexes, and the problem of non-existing complexes in the 1912 and 1913 period. Looking ahead, problems concerning forms and non-existent complexes are among the things that cause Russell to abandon the *Theory of Knowledge* manuscript.

Conclusion

In the preceding pages I have examined what I believe to be the most important strands contributing to the emergence and development of the multiple relation theory of judgement, the doctrine that proves to be the focus of Wittgenstein's attack on the *Theory of Knowledge* and the cause of its demise. I rejected interpreting Russell's turn away from objective propositions as due to his discomfort with the implications of the theory for a doctrine of truth and falsity; rather, on my view, other pressures, primarily the Liar paradox, induce him to eliminate objective false (and by parity, true) propositions and the theory of incomplete symbols gives him the means. In the context of examining why Russell replaces his doctrine of objective true and false propositions with the multiple relation theory of belief and how that shift coincides with a new interest in psychological acts like belief, I argued that the multiple relation theory is the end result of a series of attempts to solve logical and epistemological paradoxes of propositions; in Russell's attempts to solve these difficulties by means of belief, a subject for study for him under Meinong's influence, belief occurs in other roles than the role it has in his mature theory of supplying the supplement to sentences, taken as incomplete symbols. Several themes or problems emerge from his manipulations of belief: the reduction of false or negative propositions to states of disbelief, the problem of the content of false belief if belief is constituted by objects, and the attempt to provide content to belief by explaining it as a relation among ideas. These themes provide an important background to the use of belief as a supplement to sentences, and they reappear in muted or pronounced ways in the *Theory of Knowledge*. Yet the above account is still far from giving a complete picture of the emergence of the multiple relation theory of judgement, and the next chapter therefore examines how specific developments within the doctrine – changes concerning the sense and form of judgements, and changes in Russell's conception of a proposition – occur in the *Theory of Knowledge*.

Chapter 2

The Nature of the Proposition

Introduction

In Chapter 1, I considered the emergence of Russell's multiple relation theory of judgement, showing how Russell eliminates propositions as single entities by means of his doctrine of incomplete symbols, thereby opening up the possibility of explaining propositions in terms of belief. Russell employs more than one approach to eliminating propositions in this period, however, and belief, which is also coming under scrutiny as a single entity, serves in different capacities in these various approaches to eliminating propositions. The motivation for eliminating propositions – and also beliefs – as single entities comes, I argued, from Russell's need to resolve paradoxes affecting propositions. The notion of belief he uses and the very fact that he now examines belief, a psychological notion, comes, however, from his immersion in and attraction to Meinong's philosophy, with its strong bent towards descriptive psychology. Having struggled with several approaches to the paradoxes of propositions (and other paradoxes as well, which I do not examine), Russell's solution, by 1910, is to combine a theory of types (and his distinction of judging acts into elementary and general kinds) with a doctrine on which phrases (sentences) purportedly denoting propositions are incomplete symbols completed by a cognitive act of judging. After examining how the theory connects with Russell's doctrine of acquaintance, I examined how it raises difficulties for him in explaining the difference in sense of judgements containing the same items in the same form, and I described how Russell's doctrine of direct perception of complexes is used as the basis of self-evident judgements. The chapter concluded by showing how the notion of logical form is moving into the foreground of

Russell's thought, though in the case of non-existent complexes it raises problems that Russell wishes to leave to Wittgenstein to solve.

The present chapter looks for signs of Wittgenstein's impact on those parts of the *Theory of Knowledge* composed between 21 May and 26 May. This period is crucial for determining the nature of Wittgenstein's objections and for grasping the fate of the text as a whole. Russell begins work on *Theory of Knowledge* on 7 May and by 20 May has completed the first chapters of part one of his book. He is on the verge of beginning part two, which is to start with a chapter on relations, when Wittgenstein visits again to dissuade him from the project. Writing to Lady Ottoline the next day, Russell mentions how Wittgenstein came by to deliver a 'refutation' of a theory of judgement Russell 'used to hold' and observes that the refutation is 'right' but that 'the correction required is not very serious'.[1] Of course Russell wouldn't feel obliged to make a decision about how best to respond to Wittgenstein's objection unless the objection to the theory he 'used to hold' applied to his new one as well, and it is for this reason that he continues, 'I shall have to make up my mind within a week, as I shall soon reach [the chapter on] judgement'.[2] But this letter is misleading, as in fact Russell does a great deal more to address Wittgenstein than what he suggests he will do in his letter to Ottoline on the 20th.

He doesn't wait until the chapter on judgement, for one thing: Russell's attempt to explain the sense of a relation already shows signs of his dialogue with Wittgenstein, and his discussion of our understanding of logical data illustrates the important role *form* already plays in his thought. Moreover, presumably after reflection on his conversation with Wittgenstein, he decides to make other, more ambitious changes to the direction of the text, telling Ottoline on the 24th about having discovered a 'quite new' and more 'searching' way of dividing the subject of judgement.[3] On my reconstruction, on the verge of his direct response to Wittgenstein's refutation of his theory of judgement, Russell decides to introduce a sense in which the proposition is objective but logically neutral, neither affirmative nor negative, thereby taking a step towards a (bipolarity) theory of propositions. Thus despite what he says in his letter to Ottoline on the 20th, Russell does not respond to

Wittgenstein when he reaches a chapter on judgement: we do not even find such a chapter but find instead one on the nature of understanding and the nature of the proposition. This is a significant shift, and I think it responds to the larger context of Wittgenstein's objections rather than the specific refutation. But the chapter on understanding includes a specific new doctrine that qualifies, I believe, as the 'not very serious' correction Russell tells Ottoline he will have to make. That correction is to emphasize the role and importance of form in his analysis of the nature of understanding. A host of problems surround the question of whether Russell introduces form – or manipulates his use of it – to address Wittgenstein's objections, and I therefore turn to that before examining the *Theory of Knowledge.*

The Role of Form and the Nature of Wittgenstein's 20 May 'Refutation'

The difficulty in reconstructing Wittgenstein's remarks on the 20th and Russell's response can be put rather simply: since an obvious novelty in the chapter on understanding is a theory of propositions that includes form as an element alongside the terms and relation, it is natural to wonder whether this is the correction Russell predicts he will make and whether Wittgenstein's 20 May objection had to do with the need to address a proposition's form. Eames argues that the version of theory that includes form occurs first in *Theory of Knowledge* and that Russell's use of form there exemplifies his tendency to respond to Wittgenstein by using more complicated ways of symbolizing judging and relations.[4] But if Russell already embraced the theory of judgement appearing in the manuscript before he wrote the relevant chapter of his manuscript, then it follows that his response in *Theory of Knowledge* to Wittgenstein's 20 May objection involves something other than form, in which case Wittgenstein's objections were probably of some other kind as well.

There are good reasons on both sides of the issue. One reason for believing Russell added form only after meeting with Wittgenstein on the 20th is the existence among Russell's working notes of a sketch in which Russell depicts judgement and omits form.[5] The editor's (Blackwell and Eames) think these sketches depict Russell's multiple relation theory of judgement at a stage prior to the form-containing version of that doctrine presented in the *Theory of Knowledge*. Blackwell and Eames conclude from the absence of form the illustration of a multiple relation theory belonging to an early stage of writing the manuscript; further, they view these sketches as evidence that Russell added form to his analysis of judging while writing the *Theory of Knowledge*, not before. As Griffin points out, however, a reason for thinking Russell has already added form is that the notion of form is not new to 1913 but is already prominent in Russell's 1912 notes 'What is Logic?'[6] Indeed, as we saw in Chapter 1, the analysis Wittgenstein makes in his January 1913 letter seems already to introduce form, so that even if Russell did not author the idea, it would be familiar to him. Moreover, as Griffin notes, the introduction of form into judgement is too prominent to count as a small correction, nor does Russell wait till judgement to introduce it but instead form pervades the second part of his text, playing several roles.

Griffin concludes that Russell had already adopted form into his theory by the date of Wittgenstein's visit, but his point about the prominence of form in Russell's work suggests a third view, which draws on what is right in both of these alternatives. It is possible, and I think likely, that Russell has already begun to put form to use to support the theory of judgement, especially with respect to the problem of what we understand when a belief is false – and in what sense the unity of items judged actually takes place – and that he has done so before Wittgenstein meets him on the 20th. In fact it is precisely this use of form, as joined to a theory of understanding, that appears in his chapters on relations and logical data, and it is the centrality of the notion to his discussion in these chapters that has led people like Griffin to think that form must already be a component of his theory of judgement (for even Russell could not integrate a new idea that thoroughly into the rest of his system in a matter of days). While these chapters show that Russell is using form to explain how we understand relation words and logical words and sentences, they do not show him placing form explicitly within the analysis of propositions, as he does in his chapter on understanding.

As I see it, Russell responds to Wittgenstein in his chapter on under-standing by adding form to his analysis of the proposition, and he thinks of this as a small correction precisely because it has already become prominent in his attempt, prior to the 20th, to address the flaws in his 1912 theory of judgement by means of a doctrine of understanding.

Whatever correction Russell has already made to his theory of judgement must be one that is still vulnerable to Wittgenstein's refutation. I believe that Russell has already begun to rely on a theory of forms in order to address the flaws in his 1912 doctrine, and that his meeting with Wittgenstein on the 20th persuades him he has not gone far enough and he needs to make form an explicit component of the proposition and not merely an additional doctrine. This is borne out by the text. Early in his chapter on judgement Russell notes that his 1912 analysis of judgement leaves no account of how a belief can be false, and he responds to this issue by arguing that we possess an 'idea' of the objects and we suppose them to be united in a particular form. If I am correct, this is not new to *Theory of Knowledge* but predates it: in mentioning it, Russell is getting us up to speed, that is, showing us his theory as he has been rethinking it prior to the 20th. Since Russell has already begun to use form to support his theory of how we understand when we judge, he therefore is speaking the truth when he says the 1912 version of the theory of judgement, which does not address understanding as a separate issue or use form, is one he 'used to hold'. But at the same time he must be aware that his use of form needs further work, and in the attempt to solidify his account, he integrates the notion of form into his analysis of the understanding complex.

In reconstructing events like this I am taking a stand on which version of the theory of judgement Wittgenstein attacks during his 20 May visit, for by 1913 Russell has experimented with several versions of his multiple relation theory of judgement; as we saw in Chapter 1, versions of it date from 1906, 1910 and 1912. Griffin suggests that Wittgenstein's target was Russell's 1910 theory of belief,[7] since Wittgenstein's remark in the *Notebooks* that a relation is not a 'substantive'[8] is evidently linked to Russell's 1917 note added to his reprinted paper 'Knowledge by Acquaintance and Knowledge by Description' that his 1910 version of judgement is 'unduly simple'.[9] While I grant that these remarks are related, I believe Wittgenstein objected to Russell's 1912 version. Aside from the reconstruction given above, there are superficial indications. To begin with, two weeks prior to Wittgenstein's 'refutation', he learned of Russell's planned book on epistemology and visited him to express his disapproval, thinking that the text would repeat themes in the much-despised *Problems*.[10] Wittgenstein's preoccupation with the *Problems* suggests that he has it in mind on 20 May when he visits Russell with a 'refutation' of a theory of judgement that Russell 'used to hold'.

Less superficial is the nature of the difference between the 1912 and 1910 theories. In 1910 the subordinate relation (e.g. *loves* in 'Othello believes that Desdemona loves Cassio') enters with a sense, but in 1912 it does not and the cognitive act of judging distinguishes between senses.[11] Because judging arranges entities into complexes and takes responsibility for generating the proposition 'a loves b' rather than 'b loves a' the 1912 theory places more of a burden on cognitive acts of judging than does the 1910 theory, that is, it makes asserting, judging, etc. critical to the meaning of a proposition. In so doing, Russell exacerbates a feature of his theory, the fact that it conflates the way a relation occurs in a fact of belief with the way it occurs in an expression that has sense. In the sense in which the sub-ordinate relation (*loves* in the example above) occurs in a fact, it will not occur when the belief is false, whereas in the sense in which a relation occurs in a symbol for what is believed, it will continue to relate the items even when the belief is false. The effect on Russell's doctrine of judgement is to leave us in the dark as to how judge-ments can be false. Added to his doctrine that judging unifies the belief into a determinate sense, the further impact is to make it impossible to see how beliefs can be meaningful if false, since if the terms of the judgement are not arranged by judging, the judgement is meaningless and fails to express anything at all, but if they are, the judgement is true. Finally, the theory complicates rather than sim-plifies the account of sense, for judgements containing the same ingredients but expressing different senses correspond, if true, to different facts, and yet the theory seems to explain sense differences in an entirely subjective way.

By taking Wittgenstein to be critical of the 1912 version I am suggesting a particular reading of his refutation on the 20th, namely, that it concerns the tendency to bridge the way in which a relation occurs in a fact of believing with that in which it occurs in a proposition. Thus if Wittgenstein focuses on the 1912 version of Russell's theory of judgement, he is likely to worry that it hasn't produced a proposition or sense that is independent of judging, and he is likely to fault it for failing to explain how a judgement can be meaningful and false. But Wittgenstein's impulse to locate a proposition or sense – and his emerging conception of the two polarities, asserting and denying, essential to a proposition – is wedded to his fundamental idea that there are no logical constants, e.g. that 'not' is not the name of an object. These facts suggest to me that Wittgenstein appeared on the 20th demanding to know how Russell's 1912 theory permits there to be a proposition or a sense that is independent of cognitive acts of assertion or denial, and refuting the theory on the grounds that it can't explain how there is a proposition – a unity – when the subordinate relation doesn't hold. On my reading, Russell thinks that Wittgenstein's refutation, that is, the problem of false belief for his theory, is 'not too serious' and that some manipulation of his theory of forms will resolve it. Wittgenstein's larger claim – that there must be something, a proposition, prior to acts of affirming and denying, since whatever concerns the fact of believing is not relevant to the proposition – nevertheless influences Russell's subsequent decision to introduce a proposition by means of a logically neutral act of understanding.

20–21 May: 'On the Acquaintance . . . Relations'

After meeting with Wittgenstein,[12] Russell turns to drafting a chapter on the nature of our acquaintance with relations, a task that occupies him for the next two days. The chapter is important in two ways: first, to the fate of the project – in it Russell introduces analyses whose difficulties he only later sees – and second, to our understanding of Wittgenstein's objections, for wittingly or not, in his discussion of relations Russell draws attention to many of what appear to be Wittgenstein's concerns.

In general, what lies in the background of Russell's discussion reflecting Wittgenstein's concerns is doubt as to the kind of knowledge – empirical or non-empirical – expressed in statements about relations. This point is connected to the status of relations, and the suggestion in this chapter that a relation cannot be named seems to echo Wittgenstein's conviction, nascent in his January letter, that a relation isn't like a term, i.e. something we can name, though it looks like one. In addition, Russell's analysis of our knowledge of relations focuses attention on the identity criteria of sentences having the same truth-conditions (i.e. verified and falsified in the same cases). As we saw in Chapter 1, by equating the meaning of a word with an object denoted by the word, in the *Principles of Mathematics* and other early works Russell embraces a doctrine in which phrases and sentences may differ – because they are about different entities – even though they have the same truth-conditions. An example of this in the *Principles* is that words like 'before' and 'after' are said to differ in their meanings and not merely linguistically.[13] In contrast, in *Theory of Knowledge* Russell treats cases like 'a before b' and 'b after a' as the same in meaning, and though he shows no desire to abandon the doctrine of meaning he embraces in *Principles*, his analysis in effect weakens the assumption that sentences true under the same conditions may differ because they are about different entities.[14]

Russell needs to supply a positive doctrine to explain his position on a relation and its converse, and in arriving at such a theory he chooses between two alternatives, one that employs the notion of form and another that analyses relations into a conjunction of complexes. Should he account for our knowledge of asymmetrical relations in terms of acquaintance with the form of a complex or explain it in more complicated terms invoking a new, symmetrical complex associated with the original one? Since it supposes us to have acquaintance with a form, the first approach is problematic in the case of a relation that 'never holds between any pair of terms'.[15] In 'What is Logic?' Russell worries about arriving at a form if no complex containing the relation exists,[16] but in his chapter on relations in *Theory of Knowledge* his point is that the account in terms of form fails to explain how we possess the knowledge we evidently do have of relations that never hold since their forms therefore can't be what we know by acquaintance. He therefore decides in favour of the more complicated analysis and against the theory involving forms. Ironically, this decision, which appears briefly and obscurely at the end of the chapter on relations, causes him a great deal of trouble when he reaches his chapter on truth.

What is his more complicated account? To begin with, Russell has to explain how his theory of judgement (as a relation among a subject and objects) can account for the possibility of two complexes derived from the same constituents and form.[17] On his view, no single thing underlies differences in sense; rather, two possible complexes with the same form, the same terms and the same under-lying relation, *sequence*, are distinguished from each other by each being associated with a unique complex consisting of a conjunction of two new complexes. Since his account conceives of judgement as a relation between a subject and objects in some relation, to give a complete account Russell has to differentiate between complexes, and hence judgements, arising when a relation can take terms in more than one way, as *before* does in a-before-b and b-before-a. He has already withdrawn his 1911 attempt to explain sense in terms of a relation alone, as having positions for terms built in, and he therefore has to explicate sense some other way.

On his view in the *Theory of Knowledge,* words like 'before' and 'after' are not names of distinct relations *before* and *after* but pick out the same relation. If this is true for cases like 'a is before b' and 'b is after a', whose sense is the same, then it is true in cases where the phrases – like 'a is before b' and 'b is before a' – illustrate a genuine difference in sense. But if these phrases denote the same relation, so how do their senses differ, since they evidently contain names for the same objects (a and b) and since they possess the same dual rela-tional form? Put another way, Russell concedes that 'a before b' and 'b after a' have the same meaning, and this raises the question, if their meaning is the same – i.e. if they denote the same objects – how is their difference to be explained?

There is a difference between the sense of 'a is before b' and 'b is before a' because the sense of the former is determined by the complex a-earlier-and-b-later-in-the-complex, while the sense of the latter stems from the complex b-earlier-in-the-complex-and-a-later-in-the-complex. In our perception of the components of these new complexes, differences of type are conveyed; thus Russell's account relies on types of objects and our perception of them. In particular, Russell assumes we perceive the type difference between terms (like a and b) and properties (like *earlier in the complex* and *later in the complex*). Since these items are distinguishable and may comprise different conjunctive complexes, he can explain how two different senses are possible with the same constituents and form and how these possibilities can be uniquely described.

Though Russell says explicitly that sense is not a function of the relation,[18] he sometimes seems to treat sense as a function of an associated relation – here, *sequence*. But the relation does not fix sense; that claim comes too close to the view he rejects of relations containing positions for terms. Though word order distinguishes 'a before b' and 'b before a', Russell is unwilling to make order responsible for the different senses expressed by the two phrases. The phrases denote the same relation, he thinks, and a difference in the position of terms in the relation would constitute different relations. That is, if the order or position of the terms in the relation were significant, then it would be because it determines the nature of the relation. But assuming that the relation denoted is the same in both of these phrases, the order of the terms must be insignificant, merely linguistic, and irrelevant to the different senses the phrases in question express. In the case in question, the relation needing analysis is something like *sequence*, that is, something which, combined with terms like a and b – as in 'a is in a sequence with b' – possesses no particular order.

Thus sense is relative to the particular complex, and what constitutes sense is 'the relations of the constituents to the [associated] complex'.[19] This view has the following implication. Russell believes that naming is possible only when something is determinate, but on the above theory *sequence* is prior to differences in sense, which supervene on it. As I noted above, the direction of Wittgenstein's objections is towards the presuppositions of any kind of depiction or what I called the logic of depiction. Though it is likely that neither Russell nor Wittgenstein saw this aspect of his objections very clearly, it is nevertheless an undercurrent that moves Russell's thought when he attempts to address Wittgenstein's comments. Here, that undercurrent appears in Russell's attempt to get at what lies behind the possibility of difference in sense. As he states in a later chapter, his analysis of the sense of asymmetrical relations implies that we can describe the relation, that is, grasp it as it occurs in some complex or other, but not name it, for apart from occurring in these contexts, it has no determinate sense at all. Later in the *Theory of Knowledge* Russell defines the truth of judgements asserting asymmetrical relations in terms of the associated complexes he introduces here, and at the same time he acknowledges that judgements of asymmetrical relations cannot be treated as names of the truth-making complex.

At the start of the chapter on relations Russell raises and dismisses the question whether complexes and facts are the same, noting that there is, in any event, a one–one correspondence between the fact asserted by a judgement and the complex verifying it:

> It may be questioned whether a complex is or is not the same as a 'fact', where a 'fact' may be described as what there is when a judgement is true, but not when it is false.[20]

As I explained in Chapter 1, the correspondence of complex and asserted fact permits the transition from direct perception and naming of a complex to the assertion of a complex in a belief. In addition, the perception and naming of a complex is the basis on which Russell explains truth and our knowledge of truth. The doctrine that a complex exists and corresponds to the fact asserted in judging is problematic, and Russell will have great difficulty defending it in his chapter on truth and on judgements of analysis. But there is another problem: Russell's willingness to allow propositions to contain other propositions treats the imbedded proposition as if it named a fact. But in the belief statement, propositions occur differently than they do when they are asserted; they occur as something mentioned, to use modern jargon. Russell's treatment blurs that distinction, however, so that the imbedded proposition seems to play the role of asserting a fact and being named. The problem is mentioned in Wittgenstein's 'Notes on Logic':

> Frege said 'propositions are names'; Russell said 'propositions correspond to complexes'. Both are false; and especially false is the statement 'propositions are names for complexes'.[21]

Wittgenstein will later reflect on the metaphysical urge to conflate what can be said with what can be named when he writes, '[i]f a proposition is true then *Something* exists'.[22]

22–23 May: 'Logical Data'

I noted above that Russell doesn't wait till judgement to introduce the notion of form and that form pervades the second part of his text, playing several roles. This is the case when he turns to our understanding of logical data. What emerges powerfully from his discussion of our knowledge of logical data is Russell's reliance on ideas coming from Gestalt psychology, and, to a lesser degree, his use of evolutionary psychology. His use of these ideas carries his thought along channels that are arguably in tension with some of his statements of his doctrine of acquaintance as a species of knowledge involving no knowledge *that*, i.e. no propositional knowledge about a thing.

Russell turns from our perception of relations to consider our perception of 'predicates', his characteristic word for properties. I will not dwell on his discussion of properties as he merely repeats doctrines discussed in detail, for example, in his 1911 paper 'On the Relation of Universals and Particulars', concluding that there is nothing in the way of assuming a special kind of acquaintance with predicates over and above perception of relations. His discussion of our knowledge of logical data is of greater interest and concerns two related questions: How do we understand the meaning of atomic and molecular sentences; that is, with what are we acquainted when we understand a sentence? How do we understand the meaning of words; that is, what sort of acquaintance must we have in order to explain our grasp of words' meanings?

Wittgenstein visits again after Russell completes his analysis of our acquaintance with properties and before he turns to our acquaintance with logical data, but the substance of their meeting is unknown. Whether as a result of the meeting or not, Russell's discussion of our acquaintance with logical data illustrates several features of his view of logic that are anathema to Wittgenstein, and at the same time several issues begin to take on greater importance. One issue on which he and Wittgenstein diverge is the question of the nature of logic and the nature of propositions purporting to analyse other propositions. On Wittgenstein's view there is nothing in common to the logic underlying depiction and what underlies empirical propositions. Russell makes no such distinction, talking about the meaning of words like 'particular' as though in doing so he is simply engaging in something more abstract than talking about the meaning of the word 'red'. His insistence (in this chapter and the two previous) that such words and the sentences containing them belong to different types may be his attempt to speak to Wittgenstein's discomfort, but if so it fails completely. A related issue is the nature of logical constants. As I said above, I believe that on 20 May Wittgenstein refutes Russell's theory of judgement on the grounds that it fails to explain false belief and to give a proposition a sense independent of assertion and negation. I linked the demand for sense to Wittgenstein's 'fundamental' idea that there are no logical constants, e.g. that 'not' is not the name of an object. Though he is still a chapter away from fulfilling his obligation to respond to Wittgenstein's refutation, Russell's insistence that logic contains no particular constituents anticipates that issue.[23]

Yet Russell denies that logical forms are objects in order to avoid a regress ensuing if the form of a complex is taken to be a constituent alongside other terms and relations, and his reasoning here points towards another concern of the chapter: how Russell weds his conception of form as emerging by substitution of entities for other entities within a complex to a doctrine of perception. We have already seen Russell account for logical form as the abstract fact after a process of substituting increasingly general concepts for particular ones. The epistemological partner to that doctrine exploits a central concept in Gestalt psychology: the notion that we perceive things against a background, which may itself become an item in the foreground.

What acquaintance is involved in our understanding of sentences? To understand 'Socrates precedes Plato' is both to know that 'precedes' is asserted of Socrates and Plato and to be aware of the form something-somehow-related-to-something. In fact, understanding 'Socrates precedes Plato' presupposes awareness of the form. In the sense that the content of peripheral awareness, form, is not an object of acquaintance, but a condition of acquaintance, form is present in and an element of our understanding of the sentence without being another constituent. It makes sense to include form, then, in an analysis of judgement, as Russell shortly will make explicit. I have earlier touched on the question when Russell introduces the notion that form is an element in an analysis of judgement. One reason for holding, as I do, that his adoption of this view precedes the manuscript is the degree to which his epistemology is already developed in that direction. This item is so well integrated into his other doctrines as to make it unlikely to be something hastily grafted onto his system.

Since his concern in this part of the text is atomic forms, molecular forms do not get extended treatment. Nevertheless some of his comments here as well as brief remarks in notes from the period indicate the trajectory of his thought and that he is prepared to argue that, like atomic forms, molecular forms involving *and, or, not* can come to our attention by abstracting from a particular sentence.[24] Russell takes care to deny that such logical constants or forms are entities in the sense of constituents of complexes. As in the case of atomic forms, 'though they might seem to be entities', such logical constants 'are really concerned with pure form'.[25] Though not constituents of a complex, such forms are objective and presupposed by our grasp on particular molecular sentences, since, for example, when we understand the conjunctive sentence 'the sun is shining and the grass is dry', our grasp on its meaning presupposes a grasp on the abstract form some-proposition-and-some-other. Perhaps Russell hoped to extend a similar analysis to explain the connection between sentences, since he suggests in notes that our grasp on complexes involves 'inferential consciousness'.[26] These remarks are, however, quite sketchy.

What acquaintance is involved in our understanding of words? Russell's account of our understanding of sentences in terms of our awareness of the forms of the complexes corresponding to them applies to his doctrine of our grasp on word meaning. Consider our words for 'particulars, universals, relations, dual complexes, [and properties]'.[27] On his view understanding the meaning of the word 'red' as it occurs in the sentence 'this patch is red' requires having acquaintance with a particular red sense datum while presupposing some awareness of the meaning of the more abstract word 'particular'. Put more prosaically, part of what is involved in knowing what a word means is knowledge of the type of the object that gives a word its meaning. As in the case of the forms of complexes corresponding to sentences, we may bring such meanings forward and possess acquaintance with them by telescoping attention outward to survey a further condition of an object, its logical type. It is, Russell believes, a psychological fact that it is more difficult to bring logical objects and forms into the foreground and be acquainted with them than it is to grasp non-logical ones. Since the ability to grasp abstractions occurs only at a certain stage of psychological development, and Russell assumes human groups exist at various stages of such development, it follows that grasping the meaning of logical words is only possible for human groups that have achieved a fairly high level of intellectual development and is not possible among more primitive groups.

24–26 May: 'The Understanding of Propositions' (False Belief and Sense)

A theory of judgement ought to leave room for something like a proposition or sense, the sort of thing we understand even if we don't know what verifies the judgement when it is true. Russell's theory of judgement is vulnerable to the accusation that it fails to provide us with a proposition or sense, as is evident in two cases: when a judgement is false and when it asserts an asymmetrical relation. Russell's goal in his chapter on understanding is to address this complaint by showing that his theory can generate propositions from acts of understanding, and that these are prior to and presupposed by acts of judgement asserting or denying the proposition. To achieve this goal he will derive an objective proposition from the cognitive fact formed from the relation of understanding. Since he takes understanding to involve neither assertion nor denial, by generating a logically neutral proposition from it, Russell evidently hopes to avoid any suggestion that the proposition, the sense of a judgement, contains logical constants. To be persuasive his new account has to respond to the apparent failure of his theory of judgement in the case of false belief and in the case of asymmetrical relations. As it turns out, he isn't able to give a satisfactory account of either issue, and within days of propounding the doctrine of propositions as generalization of cognitive relations, he concedes its inadequacy as well.

Here he addresses the problem of false belief and the problem of sense in the following way. First, reflecting on the issue of the content of a false judgement, Russell notes that he formerly held that what united the terms was the sense of the cognitive relation of judging. As we saw in Chapter 2, this is the view he proposed in 1912. The theory makes it difficult to explain how false judgements are possible since the act of judging relates the items judged but a judgement is true when the relation it asserts to hold between terms does hold between them. Moreover, for Russell, whose rejection of idealism is both well established and total, what facts there are must be independent of our judgements, and his 1912 theory suggests the opposite. I have already said that the 1912 theory is the one Russell 'used to hold' to which Wittgenstein addresses his May 20th 'not too serious' refutation, by noting that the theory fails to account for anything like a proposition or sense, and that this is shown by the difficulties it faces accounting for the content of false belief and the different senses of asymmetrical relations.

I have already argued that prior to Wittgenstein's visit on 20 May Russell modified his 1912 theory in the direction of a theory of form, though without yet introducing form as an ingredient in the judging complex. What he failed to do in his 1912 doctrine was to explain the content of belief when the complex is not given and when our belief can be false.[28] Russell's pre-Wittgenstein correction, recorded in this chapter, attempts to show how that uniting takes place. Since the unity cannot take place in reality, acquaintance with the fact won't do, and it must be that 'what we have is the "idea" or "sugges-tion" of the terms being united in such a complex'.[29] He is not suggesting that judgement is a relation of ideas – in fact the presence of quote marks – 'idea' and 'suggestion' – show his discomfort with that version of his theory. While he cannot have been embracing a full-blown theory of judgement as a nexus of ideas, Russell seems to have been willing, in this interim theory, to say that when we judge objects to be in some relation we also imagine them in that relation, and this act of mentally holding objects up to a template, the form, provides us with belief content 'where the actual complex is not given' and 'we are concerned with a proposition which may be false'.[30] Form is involved in this act of imagining; that is, to think of terms having some relation we need to have some grasp on the form of the relation 'and this, evidently, requires that the general form of the merely supposed complex should be given'.[31]

As Russell saw when Wittgenstein met him on the 20th, his revised theory, of which the younger man is ignorant, is still vulnerable to Wittgenstein's refutation, as it remains unclear how having an idea of terms as occurring in a complex helps to explain what constitutes false belief and explains the difference senses of asymmetrical relations. What needs to be explained is how the items comprising the judgement are united in a form so as to give it sense even when it's false. Moreover, his use of quotes shows us how uncomfortably close he feels he is to a theory of ideas, a tactic he employed as early as 1906 to solve the same difficulty facing him here, what constitutes false beliefs. For though he has for some time viewed judgement as dealing in objects and not ideas, his revision, now under examina-tion, comes extremely close to reverting to the earlier view, for it appears to claim that the mental arrangement of (ideas of) the objects comprising judgement provides the judgement's sense and content. If I am correct, Russell has already adopted a background theory of form to augment his account of judgement – one that conveys a disturbingly subjective impression by its use of ideas of objects in a form. This is compatible with seeing form as new to

Russell's doctrine as an explicit feature of his analysis of under-standing. That is, in the present chapter, his 'not too serious' cor-rection is to imbed form within the multiple relation, so that instructions as to the sense of the judgement are, so to speak, written into the act of judging itself. Russell doesn't explain this new move, however, until he introduces propositions in another section of the chapter. Rather he turns to the second difficulty: our understanding of the differences in sense that arise from asymmetrical relations.

Russell has already shown how to distinguish between complexes containing the same terms, relation and form. For example, he dis-tinguished between the complex a-before-b and the complex b-before-a by means of a proposition, 'there is a complex g in which a precedes and b succeeds'.[32] All he needs to do here is to show the connection between that account, which depends on defining new complexes associated with the original, and his theory of under-standing. To understand 'a is before b' is to understand 'there is a complex γ in which a is earlier and b is later', that is, it is to under-stand a proposition conjoining atomic propositions. No one could claim to understand this, however, in the way he recommends if 'a is earlier in γ and b is later in γ' could be understood in two senses. Neither could one could claim understanding if disambiguating 'a is earlier in γ and b is later in γ' led to a regress of analyses. Noting that 'a is earlier in γ and b is later in γ' is a conjunction of two atomic propositions, Russell argues that since its atomic conjuncts have the 'form of dual complexes consisting of a simple and a complex', and simples and complexes 'differ logically',[33] their transposition is blocked and no alternative proposition 'γ is earlier in a' can arise.[34] Since no ill effect arises from changing the order of the conjuncts, and since understanding cannot differentiate 'a before b' from 'b before a' in terms of elements and form alone,[35] Russell views the introduction of molecular propositions as unavoidable. In a matter of days, he concedes that understanding a false proposition con-cerning an asymmetrical relation implies the existence of a false con-junction and hence the existence of false propositions as conjuncts.

Following Sommerville, Eames suggests that Russell's claim above is what annoyed Wittgenstein, what he said he had tried – presum-ably the attempt referred to in the January letter – and knew wouldn't work.[36] In other words, Wittgenstein is thought to have given up an attempt to preserve sense by means of treating simples and complexes as different in type. Wittgenstein's January letter arguably asserts that Russell's analysis has made it possible for there to be propositions which express type-mistakes precisely because it has *not* shown that these items differ logically.[37] Sommerville argues that in that letter, complexes were supposed to join with terms in such a way that the analysis can't make type mistakes. But, Wittgenstein realized, nothing is gained by introducing a complex if the type difference between a complex and a term is lost, in so far as they are both treated as objects and named. Russell nevertheless believes that analysis to be impervious to nonsense combinations and that difficulties in sense are irrelevant to discovering what 'understanding a proposition' means.

Finally, I noted above that one reason for believing Russell added form only after meeting with Wittgenstein on the 20th is the existence among Russell's working notes of a sketch in which Russell depicts judgement and omits form.[38] The sketch in question appears below.

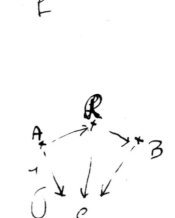

Figure 2. *Diagram of judgement (without form)*[39]

As Blackwell and Eames point out, in the top sketch Russell depicts an arrow leading from A to B, using the letter 'L' to indicate the asymmetrical *left of* and indicating the sense of the relation by an arrow. He then depicts that complex's incorporation into judgement, using 'S' for the subject, 'J' for *judging*, and 'L' (over-written with 'R') for the subordinate relation.[40] More important, to my view, is the presence of relations with sense and the fact that R is a term related to other terms in judging but not in the complex. The editors notice that in the upper sketch Russell indicates the sense of the relation by the direction of the arrow, but they fail to notice that Russell incorporates sense in the judging fact too, by means of the same device of horizontal arrows. Both *love* and *judges* exhibit sense in this sketch, and in *Theory of Knowledge* Russell denies that relations possess sense; thus, as we saw, the relation *judging* cannot confer sense, contrary to his suggestion in 1912. The fact that the diagrams display judgement in a way vulnerable to the critique Russell makes of his 1912 theory of judgement and the revised version of it suggests that he may have drafted them while writing that portion of the chapter. Though the existence of the sketch above does not show Russell's intent in drafting it, alongside other diagrams (shown below), such as drafts of the sketch that occurs in the text, and that sketch itself, the existence of the sketch above suggests that Russell is focusing on how form can resolve the problem of the content of belief, the sense or proposition, especially when the belief is false – and that he inserts form to address that issue.

24–26 May: 'The Understanding of Propositions' (the Nature of the Proposition)

When Russell told Ottoline he would have to address Wittgenstein's 20 May criticism of his theory of judgement, he has in mind this part of the text. But by the time he reaches the stage in his writing dealing with cognitive relations involving multiple objects, he has refined his original plan for this stretch of text. Russell's contemplation of the problem of false belief may have suggested to him a much more ambitious undertaking, one which involves dividing the subject according to different ways propositions occur, in cognitive contexts such as belief or disbelief and in ostensibly cognitively neutral contexts such as *understanding* or *supposition*. If something like this sequence is the case, it means that though Russell originally only plans to address Wittgenstein's specific objection with a specific response (the introduction of a theory of ideas explained below), he ultimately responds to the broader implications of that objection as well. In a letter to Ottoline on the 24th reporting that he is now writing on judgement and that he has made an abstract of the text, Russell relays having had new, important ideas and discovered a 'quite new' and more 'searching' way of dividing the subject of judgement.[41] I agree with the editors of the *Theory of Knowledge* that the abstract Russell mentions to Ottoline came bundled with the manuscript as a sheet of paper with an outline of the second part of the text on one side and diagrams of the multiple relation of understanding prefiguring those in the chapter in question on the other.[42] On the outline Russell asks whether propositions belong to epistemology or logic, an interesting shift from his view in 'What is Logic?' and other work prior to *Theory of Knowledge* that propositions belong entirely within epistemology.[43] I argue that the new division of the subject is reflected in Russell's decision to distinguish between propositions that involve acts of neutral understanding (and hence sense but no affirmation or negation, truth or falsity) and propositions that occur in the context of affirmation and negation (and bring in truth or falsehood). This division spans two chapters, with the discussion of affirmation and negation (truth and falsity) occurring in a later chapter.

The central question in the chapter on understanding – whether 'we can give a definition of a "proposition" which neither brings in anything mental nor makes the proposition an incomplete symbol'[44] – speaks to the worry that his theory is unduly subjective. In doing so, however, he is reconfirming and not rejecting his doctrine that belief completes incomplete symbols and gives them meaning. The problem is that it gives them too much subjective meaning. Thus 'that this is red' is a meaningless phrase; it expresses a proposition in the sense in which a proposition is an incomplete symbol, and it is only in the context of assertion or such other mental context that 'the phrase expressing a proposition acquires a complete meaning'.[45] But a doctrine that accepts only incomplete symbols and psychological acts that give the symbols meaning seems inadequate so long as he hasn't shown how the proposition or sense is objective and independent of psychological contexts. A *proposition* is described in a preliminary way as what is common to different attitudes, that is, their meaning.[46] Phrases like 'I believe it's cold outside' or 'you perceive it's cold outside' record psychological states and exhibit 'the sort of difference between two phrases . . . not concerned with the objects in themselves, but only with their relation to the subject'.[47] That is, the very mechanism enabling an act of believing, doubting and so on to flesh out 'that this is red' into 'I believe this is red' and 'I doubt this is red' draws the proposition into an essential relationship with a subject, and this explains why he thinks such acts fail to provide objective propositions.

In part one of *Theory of Knowledge*, in the context of defending against neutral monism his mind/body dualism – specifically, the existence of mental entities like the logical subject – Russell notes that judgement is an occurrence or fact having an essential reference to the subject or judge. Different people, or the same person at different times, may, in believing, address the same content, but in the act of believing that content comes into relation with a particular mental entity, the believer, and a particular moment, the moment the belief occurs. For example, an abstract mathematical truth is non-temporal – it is not a dated event, occurring sometimes but not other times – but when I understand one, I relate it with a temporal particular – a moment in time – and make the abstract truth into a dated event. By means of 'the intermediary of some extraneous temporal particular' the proposition $2 + 2 = 4$ acquires 'the special relation to certain moments which is involved in its being sometimes thought of and sometimes not'.[48] In believing that $2 + 2 = 4$ we introduce an essentially subjective element 'not involved in the object of my belief'.[49] What is relevant to the chapter on understanding propositions is not Russell's argument as to why there must be mental entities,[50] but his assumption that believing (doubting, etc.) make a thought my thought at this moment, and because this 'partly incommunicable' aspect is entirely subjective it ultimately fails to deliver a common content or proposition that is wholly objective.

As I argued above, Wittgenstein seems to have urged Russell to explain differences in sense in terms of something non-mental and prior to the differences in sense it explains. That tendency is evident in Russell's chapter on our grasp on relation words, and in discussing the nature of our grasp on the sense of propositions, the same concern manifests in a desire to isolate something objective and in common to different cognitive complexes. In his chapter on our grasp on words for relations, a sense-neutral relation *similarity* explains what is common to 'before' and 'after'. In his treatment of our grasp on expressions for propositions, the relation of *understanding* – 'a state of mind from which affirmation and negation are wholly absent' – explains what is common to and presupposed by 'asserts', 'denies', 'doubts', and so forth. Rejecting Meinong's doctrine of assumption as a state of mind involving assertion and denial,[51] Russell writes:

> It is clear that there is something which we may call 'understanding a proposition', which is presupposed equally by assertion, suggestion, doubt and volition.[52]

By defining propositions in terms of the relation of *understanding*, Russell hopes to do justice to the fact that a proposition is what is common to a variety of contexts: belief, doubt, affirmation, denial, etc. By abstracting from all the particular terms constituting the understanding fact, he hopes to arrive at something that no longer has an essential reference to a particular subject or a particular moment in time. The resulting fact or form is therefore objective, not subjective, and common to all other cognitive acts having the same form. That is, 'there is a U and an S such that U (S, x, R, y, γ)' is an objective proposition, not a mere incomplete symbol, and it is 'the same for all subjects and for all propositional relations . . . concerned with the same proposition'.[53]

The structure of most facts (e.g. a-left-of-b) can be captured in a diagram, with the relation of the elements of the diagram showing the structure of the fact. Moreover it is possible to correlate the elements of the diagram with more than one fact; indeed, it depicts any facts of the same structure. That Russell assumes a-judges-aRb is analogous to a-left-of-b is made clear by his attempt to diagram 'the logical structure of the fact, which consists in a given subject understanding a given proposition'.[54] Russell's diagram depicts the logical structure of a five-termed complex A-understands-that-a is similar to b. The diagram represents the subject A, the relation U, the subordinate relation R, the terms a and b, and the form (Figure 3).

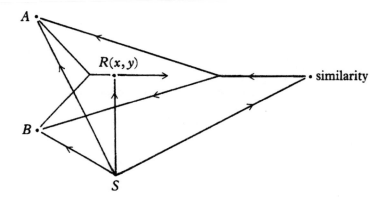

Figure 3. *Diagram in* Theory of Knowledge *of understanding (with form)*[55]

In addition to this diagram there exists a page containing two diagrams of judgement, which came bundled with the *Theory of Knowledge* manuscript, and which is in several respects comparable to the diagram occurring in the manuscript.[56] Despite the differences between Figures 3 and 4, their many shared features suggest that Figure 4 depicts a draft of the sketch that appears in the text and is displayed as Figure 3.

These diagrams are worth considering. In Figure 4, the lower sketch attempts to be three-dimensional; that is, in it Russell projects judgement over another relation, *similarity*, and its form. A occurs directly above B on a vertical plane divided by *similarity*, indicated by a horizontal line. That is, *similarity* divides the plane into A-similar-B and B-similar-A. This structure is projected into judging, where we still have *similarity*, and A and B on a vertical plane, despite the addition of the subject and other elements. If we ignore the projected parts, the bottom diagram of judgement in Figure 4 is virtually identical to the one occurring in the text. This is not true of

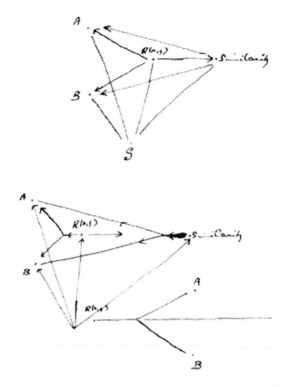

Figure 4. *Early draft of the diagram of understanding*[57]

the upper sketch in the pair, for in that sketch the arrow from the form R(x,y) to the relation *similarity* actually joins the two. The shifting representation of the connection of form to the relation may indicate that Russell wishes to show that the form is on a different level of abstraction than the relation and its terms; in any event it shows that he is reflecting on the appropriate way to depict form. In his 1918 discussion of the logical form of belief in the *Philosophy of Logical Atomism,* Russell denies that it is possible to draw a 'map in space' of belief, acknowledging Wittgenstein at this point.[58] In the fourth chapter of this study I argue that very soon after completing this chapter Russell begins to doubt whether a fact whose form is that of judgement (belief, etc.) is at all like or can be correlated with any other form of fact. Though muffled, this doubt records the point at which he begins to consider whether a proposition occurs in 'A believes that aRb' in the same way that it occurs, for example, in 'aRb v ~aRb'. As I noted in the Introduction, this line of thought leads him in the mid-1920s to admit that the way a proposition occurs in the first context has no relation with the way it occurs in the second.

Before turning to the next chapter and the fall-out of Wittgenstein's angry meeting with Russell on the 26th, it is necessary to briefly touch on some issues concerning Russell's conception of the logical subject. In the diagram above the subject is given the name 'S', yet earlier in *Theory of Knowledge* Russell goes to great lengths to deny that we can name the subject of an act of belief (understanding, etc.). Insisting that the relation of acquaintance suffices to justify his dualist doctrine of belief as a mental fact, he rejects the subject as a nameable object of acquaintance. His argument turns on his doctrine that if a relation of acquaintance occurs it must be of something and by something and on the fact that we may focus our attention on a particular and subsequently become aware of our own attention and *that* 'there is always a subject attending to the object called "this"'.[59] That is, in acquaintance with an object we also experience as a datum the *fact* that something is acquainted with the object in which the experiencing subject appears as an apparent variable, not as an individual object.[60] It follows that subjects are not known by acquaintance but only 'as referents for the relation of acquaintance and for those other psychical relations, judging, desiring, etc., which imply acquaintance'.[61] So long as there is an act of acquaintance, something relata must exist of a kind capable of justifying his belief that there are specifically mental facts, even though subjects are known only by description and cannot be named. In the later parts of the text Russell ignores this point, and when he turns to the analysis of understanding and belief, he proceeds as though expressions for belief contain names for subjects.[62] Though he may view these expressions as descriptions needing further analysis, he fails to say so or to note the need for further analysis, and the implications of his earlier argument for his analysis of mental relations is left unresolved.

Conclusion

In the preceding pages I recommend a reconstruction of Russell's important 20 May conversation with Wittgenstein and show how Russell's work on relations and logical data, that is, the work he does in the three days immediately following Wittgenstein's visit, shows signs of that meeting. I argue that Wittgenstein's ideas can be detected, despite being framed by Russell's Platonist and atomist theory of meaning, in Russell's attempt to talk about something prior to differences of sense and independent of linguistic conventions. Indeed, to suggest as he does there that a relation cannot be named strongly resonates with Wittgenstein, who suggests in January that a form together with a name might fix the significance of the proposition and who later urges that a relation looks like but isn't a substantive.[63] Despite the growing divergence in their views on the nature of logic, Wittgenstein's impact is less apparent in Russell's discussion of logical data than it is in his chapter on relations, though Russell may be responding to Wittgenstein's urging when he denies there are any logical objects. But Russell's doctrine of our knowledge of logical data has its own significance within his philosophical framework, and more than anything else his psychological and epistemological account of our grasp of logical words and sentences shows the degree to which he does not yet grasp Wittgenstein's view of logic. From Wittgenstein's perspective, the logic underlying depiction is of a completely different nature than and discontinuous from what underlies propositions that require perceptual verification; for him logic is not characterized by complete generality understood as a process of 'dematerializing' a proposition.[64]

The most important evidence of Wittgenstein's impact on Russell's work comes, as Russell says it will, when he reaches the part of the text dealing with multiple, rather than dual, relations. Russell opens that section of the text by discussing the nature of understanding, a logically neutral cognitive act that he uses to define a sense in which a proposition is objective and not merely an incomplete symbol dependent for sense on subjective acts of mind. I argued that prior to writing the manuscript he has already become dissatisfied with the ability of his 1912 theory of judgement's ability to explain what we understand when a judgement may be false and has, along with his increased emphasis on form in general, begun to use form to give an account of understanding; having already made this shift, his first response to Wittgenstein's 20 May refutation is to imbed form as a further ingredient in the analysis of the multiple relation. Yet his chapter resonates Wittgenstein's influence in larger, more diffuse ways as well, and it seems likely that his decision to analyse understanding – which is new to the text as well as to introduce a proposition independent of subjective states of mind and neither asserted nor denied shows how seriously he is taking Wittgenstein's demand for a proposition, or sense. The signs of the younger man's impact are also present in Russell's willingness to consider whether propositions belong to logic or epistemology, as well as in his decision to emphasize the transition from atomic propositions in part two to molecular propositions in part three. Though he never succeeds in reaching part three, the new division of the subject suggests that he is in some way mimicking or approximating, from within his own philosophical framework of assumptions and beliefs, Wittgenstein's conception of the emergence of molecular propositions from atomic ones.

To put it mildly, Russell's work is not well received when he shows it to Wittgenstein on the 26th. Russell later admits that he hid his anxiety over the implications of Wittgenstein's remarks at that meeting to himself, and this fact, plus Wittgenstein's incoherence on the 26th, may explain why Russell says so little that is informative in his letter to Ottoline about the quarrel. Yet in the chapters that follow this meeting – chapters that bring us to the end of Russell's work on the text – there is plenty of evidence that what Wittgenstein finds problematic in Russell's account concerns the fact that what is essential to belief is that it be about a proposition, not a complex, while what is essential to a proposition is its bipolarity. I address these issues in the following chapter.

Chapter 3

Analysis, Belief, Truth and Certainty

Introduction

In the last chapter I suggested that when Wittgenstein meets with Russell on 20 May he points out that Russell's 1912 theory of judging makes the cognitive relation of judging responsible for the sense of the judgement and therefore fails to explain the fact that we understand something, a proposition, even when we judge falsely, and what we understand is independent of assertion or denial or other acts of mind. A proposition can be used to assert or deny – both of these uses belong to it essentially – but the polarity of affirmative and negative use that is essential to a proposition is absent from Russell's theory, or at best, he introduces it as a subjective cognitive relation, external to the proposition. In addition to highlighting the bipolarity of the proposition, Wittgenstein's objection presses Russell to clarify the form of sentences like 'A believes p', anticipating his later claim that the form of 'A believes p' cannot be compared to the forms of relational complexes. In pressing towards what is unique in contexts like 'A believes p', Wittgenstein is demanding to know how statements like 'A believes p' have any bearing on the logic of propositions; he is not attempting to add a species to the classification of forms, though that is what Russell takes from him. In Chapter 2 I further argued that by 20 May and making prominent use of form Russell has already begun to build a doctrine of understanding around his 1912 theory in order to address how we understand even when judging falsely. It is for this reason, I argued, that he is sanguine about Wittgenstein's refutation on the 20th, even though he sees his new emphasis on the understanding of form will need revising as well. He subsequently decides to make form an ingredient in the judgement, a role it was already virtually occupying, given his account of how understanding involves acquaintance with forms. But this, I suggested, was not all: before Russell turns to the task of responding to Wittgenstein's refutation, he sees a new way to divide the subject, and on my reconstruction, it is at this point that he decides to introduce a sense in which the proposition is objective and prior to acts of affirmation and negation. In short, he responds to Wittgenstein by emphasizing the importance of form and taking a step towards a (bipolarity) theory of propositions.

These efforts did not win Russell any ground. We know from his letter to Ottoline that when he showed Wittgenstein a 'crucial part' of the chapter on propositions he was told that 'it was all wrong, not realizing the difficulties' and that Wittgenstein 'had in fact tried my view and knew it wouldn't work'.[1] The present chapter turns to Russell's work in the period right after receiving this second onslaught. This stretch of the text, which brings us to the close of the book, shows Russell trying to persevere in his original enterprise while acknowledging, in his writing in the text itself, numerous problems that threaten to unravel it. The chapters in question concern such topics as analysis, negation, truth and certainty, but in the context of raising these issues, numerous problems emerge, in particular, the difficulty of treating perception as a multiple relation, the content of false belief, the bipolarity of propositions and the nature of the correspondence that, he thinks, defines truth. A final theme concerns the connection between his ailing theory of judgement and the defence he makes against scepticism and solipsism.

Problems proliferate so rapidly in this portion of the *Theory of Knowledge* that a special effort of classification has to be made at the outset. Some of these difficulties do not appear to have occurred to Russell, or there is no mention of it in his writings. This is the case, for example, on the question whether his theory of judgement can continue to support his argument against solipsism. Other issues do occur to Russell, at least in his later work, and it is an open question whether he reflected on them in this period. An example is his theory of perception as a multiple relation, for as he admits in 1918 the logical form of perception, like that of belief, is problematic and requires the admission that expressions for it contain two verbs. Even when he does make explicit reference to problems with his theory of judgement – as in his account of truth – it is not necessarily the case that these lead him to abandon the text, for, as I noted above, Russell continues to view his theory of judgement as a going concern – needing fixing, to be sure, but still worthwhile – long after he abandons the text. The point of the present chapter is not to isolate his reasons for abandoning the text but to show how he struggles with Wittgenstein's objections and begins to get a better understanding of them. In the next and final chapter I look at how, in notes, Russell responds to the problems facing his theory of judgement by giving yet another analysis of propositions, an analysis that moves closer to Wittgenstein's conception of propositional bipolarity – and abandons the attempt to depict belief as relational fact or complex – but that ends, despite these concessions, in an admission of failure.

26–27 May: 'Analysis and Synthesis'

Still depressed by his interchange with Wittgenstein the day before, Russell turns on the 27th to the question of the cognition involved when we engage in the analysis of complexes into their parts and the synthesis of those parts into wholes. His discussion is based on several assumptions that we can easily imagine Wittgenstein would reject, and when, in the chapter itself, Russell notes several objections whose effect is to put pressure on these assumptions it is possible that these reflect Wittgenstein's comments on the previous day or on some earlier occasion. To begin with, Russell assumes that judgements expressing analyses have meaning and are verified in the same way as other judgements. He also believes that however many judgements may be inferred from others, some must be based on perception or else knowledge is inexplicable. Thus his account of analysis is intended to explain what objects and acts of perception account for the class of judgements that analyse complexes into their constituents.

The importance of the topic of analysis in Russell's thought in the 1910–1913 period has to do with how he sees judgements emerging from perception; his discussion of analysis is, in fact, about perception and the problems it raises are problems concerning perception.

Since the transition from perception to judging is matched at the level of language by the transition from names to judgements, Russell's doctrine is pertinent to his attempt to treat facts as things that can be named. As we saw in Chapter 1, in perceiving a complex, we are able to derive a judgement based on that perception, and this judgement of perception is theoretically if not in practice both true and self-evident. In Russell's *Principia* and in other work from 1911 and 1912, analysis receives very little separate attention as a cognitive act, though he assumes that some act of analysis links perception of simples with judgements of perception. Here analysis is made a topic of its own chapter. This is to be expected; Russell's *Theory of Knowledge* is supposed to fill in the epistemology merely sketched in *Principia* and elsewhere. Yet less expected is the fact that analysis is now positioned after a discussion of understanding instead of after perception. Russell positions his discussion of analysis here because he treats it, in the text, as involving a multiple relation of perception that like all the other kinds (belief, doubt, etc.) presupposes understanding. But by assuming the existence of a multiple relation of perception, he blurs the line between his doctrine of dual relations and his doctrine of multiple relations, and throws the notion of analysis into question. Ironically, Russell introduces the notion of perception as a multiple relation in order to avoid blurring that line. This is apparent at the outset of his chapter.

Russell defines analysis as 'the discovery of the constituents and the manner of combination of a given complex'.[2] On his account of consciousness, there is more than one way to discover the constituents of a whole but these ways need to be distinguished from analysis. For example, in attending to objects we become aware of parts but we don't perceive them *as* parts of a complex, whereas what is essential to analysis is that we know that the parts perceived are parts of a complex. Because in attending we are 'aware of what is in fact a part, . . . without making us aware of its being a part',[3] analysis, that is, knowing the perceived parts are parts of some whole, presupposes attention and is only possible only if we perceive in a manner that resists offering up further objects of attention,[4] and this requires that the parts appear to perception as related to some whole. Since information – e.g. the relevance of parts to some whole

– is clearly involved in judgement of analysis, his attempt to explain analysis begins to seem untenable, for we need to engage in analysis to get from the perceived complex to the judgement about its parts, but if the judgement of analysis doesn't rest on perception, the knowledge conveyed by it, which can't be inferred, is inexplicable:

> To analyse a given complex γ, it would seem that we must know such facts as 'a is part of γ'. But since this cannot be an inferred judgement, it must be derived from perception of the complex 'a-part-of-γ'.

In the *Tractatus*, Wittgenstein touches on this point when he notes that 'to perceive a complex means to perceive that its constituents are combined in such and such a way', but the implication of his remark is that a correct grasp on the form of perceiving and judging will be one that breaks away from an account given in terms of complexes of objects.[5] In contrast, because we do in fact engage in analysis, and because he assumes this has to have some perceptual basis, Russell concludes that the mind must be capable of acts of perception in which it stands in a multiple rather than dual relation to what is perceived. Acts like these of complex perception account for how it is that we are able to give names to what we experience in a way that we can subsequently unfold into a judgement of perception, for the names bestowed in these complex acts of perception are themselves complex (e.g. 'aRb'). Because complex perception enables us to name our experience, it resembles acquaintance, and because it has the form of a multiple relation it resembles judgement; in Russell's classification of kinds of knowledge, complex perception sits between acquaintance and judgement.[6] This point is explicit in the next chapter when Russell writes:

> In connection with analysis, we had occasion to consider a multiple relation called 'complex perception'; but although multiple, this relation had more affinities with ordinary acquaintance and with attention than with propositional thought, just because its objects were the same as those of ordinary acquaintance and attention.[7]

Both parts of Russell's account of perception, the aspect in which it resembles a dual relation and the aspect in which it resembles a multiple one, are problematic. First, by placing perception in the class of multiple relations, as having the form 'A perceives that aRb', Russell subjects perception to many of the criticisms Wittgenstein levels against his doctrine of belief, and in particular to the rebuke that perceiving must contain two relations and the subordinate relation must occur as a relation rather than as a term. Without elaborating on it, Russell acknowledges this problem in his 1918 series of lectures on logical atomism:

> This [doctrine of perception] raises also a number of logical difficulties which I do not propose to go into, but I think you can see for yourself that perceiving would also involve two [relations] just as believing does.[8]

Second, as Russell sees, to explain judgements that analyse complexes it isn't enough to say that we know the meanings of simple names; this will not give us any information about their different ways of bearing on each other in the complex – that is, it won't be enough to explain how we arrive at a judgement. But in making room in his system for acts of complex perception and complex names, Russell virtually collapses the distinction between knowledge of objects, which is supposed to be uninformative, and knowledge of truths, and between naming and judging.[9] In addition, his difficulty explaining on the basis of simple names how we are able to make analytic judgements isn't really solved by the addition of complex names, for it isn't clear that he can explain the meaning of complex names merely in terms of the meanings of their constituent simple names. Russell alludes to this problem when near the end of the chapter he reports that it is possible to ask how 'the meaning of a complex name such as "aRb" [is] determined when the meanings of the simple constituent names are known'.[10] The meaning of certain names, such as the complex name 'a-before-b', is indeterminate because the meanings of their simple constituent names (and the arrangement of those names) corresponds to more than one possible complex. But a name, complex or otherwise, has meaning only when it corresponds to something, that is, to a unique thing – that is Russell's conviction.[11] How, then, are names whose meaning is indeterminate names at all?

These tensions are consequences of Russell's atomistic doctrine of meaning, which explains the meaning of words and sentences in terms of objects and external relations. But in the present chapter and throughout the text, Russell assumes that logical (that is, onto-logical) problems can be separated from epistemological ones, and therefore tries to set these logical difficulties aside as irrelevant to his concern.[12] Besides the problem of explaining the meaning of complex names, Russell raises two other questions that, like it, reflect important themes of Wittgenstein's emerging criticism. The first question concerns the form of propositions or judgements that assert analyses, that is, what is essential to such propositions, or as Russell puts it: what is meant by 'aRb consists of a and R and b united in the general form of a dual complex'?[13] The issue is closely related to Wittgenstein's emerging objections to Russell's theory of belief, for propositions like 'A believes that p' that assert belief are only somewhat more concealed cases of propositions (like '"p" says p') that talk about propositions. Wittgenstein's question – and it seems likely that this is what we are hearing – is, I think, meant to direct attention to the radical differences between the way propositions occur in these instances and the way they occur in truth-functions. The same general intention is evident when Russell relates as another possible issue, 'how we come to know the truth of such propositions'.[14] To question how we come to know the truth of an analytic judgement is to ask whether we need to refer to empirical facts to verify them. Wittgenstein later embraces a distinction between genuine propositions that express truths or falsehoods and apparent propositions that merely reflect grammatical rules, and the presence of this question in the chapter on analytic judgements suggests that he is beginning to draw that distinction already. Put another way, the question suggests that he would say that though these judgements appear to analyse complexes, they actually only express certain grammatical rules.

Though Russell doesn't address the full force of these objections for quite some time, in a matter of days additional difficulties will surface that cast further doubt on the account he gives here of the perceptual basis of judgements of analysis.

27–28 May: 'Various Examples of Understanding'

We've already seen that Russell arranges multiple relations into a hierarchy based on the number of terms related by judging. On that view, the more variables there are in an understanding (judging, doubting, etc.) complex, the less relata there are for the cognitive relation, and the simpler it is. Logically simpler, that is: a theory of psychological shifts in attention explains the cognitive processes by means of which we alternate between general statements ('something has some relation to something') and particular statements ('Othello loves Desdemona'), and on that doctrine what is logically simple may be psychologically difficult. When Russell turns from discussing the nature and conditions of analysis to a further application of his new theory of propositions, these doctrines come into play, and the 'various examples' alluded to in the title illustrate the different levels of abstraction multiple relations may possess, from the complete generality of logical judgements to the specificity of statements of common sense. By implication, logical statements are simply generalizations of empirical ones, and they can be understood just as empirical statements can, though in the case of logical propositions the nature of understanding is simpler and more direct than it is when empirical propositions are concerned. Wittgenstein's belief that statements of logical and grammatical rules are completely unlike other statements, as 'logic must turn out to be *totally* different than any other science'[15] is clearly antagonistic to both this conception of logic and to the hierarchy of cognitive relations under examination in this chapter.

Russell's first example is the nature of our understanding of logical propositions, or, since he calls these 'forms', the nature of our understanding of forms.[16] As we saw earlier, in Russell's discussion of logical data, he reasoned that forms, that is, abstract entities like something-somehow-related-to-something, must be objects of acquaintance if they are to serve as the meanings we grasp in comprehending logical words and sentences.[17] In this chapter he

explains that it is because a general proposition, a form or completely general fact, has no particular terms and is simple that it can
be an object of acquaintance. Though Russell is comfortable saying
that the completely general proposition 'something is somehow
related to something' is simple, he is aware of and reports that his
account raises the question how something can be simultaneously
simple and a fact, that is, 'the sort of object whose reality makes a
proposition true'.[18] Assuming this question to originate in Russell's
conversation with Wittgenstein, one issue it signals has to do with the
notions 'simple' and 'complex' and the work these categories are
supposed to do. For example, in his analysis of relations, Russell
explains that wrong substitutions like 'γ is a part of the complex a'
are impossible because the two are of different types: one is simple,
the other complex. If Russell wishes to use the categories 'simple'
and 'complex' to guarantee sense – and he does – then he shouldn't
also allow it to be possible to assert significantly 'a simple is a
complex', for if that makes sense, then his defence against wrong
way substitutions falls apart. As we have seen, Russell's epistemological doctrine of perception permits something to be seen as complex
or simple, and here he is willing to fudge the difference between
simples and complexes in the case of forms. This fact no doubt
explains Wittgenstein's comment that:

> Russell's complexes were to have the useful property of being
> compounded, and were to combine with this the agreeable
> property that they could be treated as 'simples'. But this alone
> made them unserviceable as logical types, since there would
> have been significance in saying of a simple, that it was a
> complex.[19]

Because it doesn't speak to his present interest in epistemology,
Russell shows no desire to address this issue. He shows similar dis-
interest in the related problem that because his analysis defines
logical propositions in terms of a dual relation of understanding, the
'opposition of truth and falsity' has no application to the proposition being defined.[20] Similarly, though he acknowledges that if pure
forms are simples we ought to be able to name them 'John' or

'Peter', he doesn't pause even long enough to mention that what prevents us from doing so is that we must be able to prefix a logical constant like 'not' to a proposition and cannot do so to a name.[21] Indeed, the only question Russell does address is the one that concerns his epistemological hierarchy, namely, that if we assume that forms (general propositions) are simples, that we know them through a dual relation analogous to acquaintance, and so on, then there is no 'radical difference' between how we understand propositions about forms and how we understand propositions about particulars.[22] His answer is to point to the cases he is examining as evidence of the existence of different forms of understanding.

Turning to cases such as 'something is similar to something' that occur further down on the hierarchy, Russell introduces a complex of understanding as 'a three term relation of the subject, the form, and the relation'.[23] As before, understanding is supposed to define a proposition, that is, something true or false, but it seems impossible to do so when the subordinate relation in question doesn't hold, for then understanding lacks one of its relata and the proposition is incomplete. He raises this point as follows:

> It might, no doubt, be questioned whether such a proposition as 'something has the relation R to something' would have any meaning if it were false, i.e., if, in fact, there were no instances of R whatsoever.[24]

On Russell's account of propositions, the proposition (or form or fact) is generalized from entities with which we are acquainted, but if the assertion is about an entity with which we are not acquainted, how do we generalize that assertion into a form, a general fact, that is, into a self-standing proposition? Pursuing the point further, Russell notes that to assert that a relation has no instances is the same as to assert that there is a proposition asserting that relation and the proposition is false. In his words:

> [I]n saying that there are relations of which there are no instances, what we should naturally suppose that we mean would be 'there are *propositions* of the form xRy for values of R

for which such propositions are false whatever x and y may be'.[25]

These passages address two related difficulties: first, his account of propositions isn't able to generate a proposition in those cases where the relation doesn't hold, and, second, his account fails to capture what we mean by a proposition's falsity, namely, that 'a relation fails to hold'. That is, Russell can neither generate a false proposition nor explain what it means for a proposition to be false. And that is not all that's wrong with his theory, for his definition of a proposition seems to require that it be understood – i.e. that it occur in a fact of understanding – but of course a proposition is significant even if no one understands it. Concluding that his definition of a proposition is 'inadequate', Russell writes:

> It seems plain that 'aRb' has 'meaning' provided R is the right sort of entity, and the question whether R is the right sort of entity depends upon its logical character, and not upon the more or less accidental question of whether instances of it actually occur.[26]

Admitting that he has no answer to the difficulties besetting his theory of propositions, Russell wraps up the discussion of understanding by turning to propositions that assert asymmetrical relations. In his chapter on relations, Russell analysed asymmetrical relations like a-before-b into a conjunction of relations 'a is earlier in γ and b is later in γ'. In the present chapter he explains understanding in cases, like these, that involve molecular complexity in terms of acquaintance with a form, a relation (e.g. *before*), and the term or terms. To arrive at the form he ignores the conjunction as a whole and looks at its parts, the complex a-earlier-in-γ and the complex b-later-in-γ. In both of these cases, the form is that of a dual complex 'consisting of a simple and a complex'.[27] Since simples and complexes are different types and rearranging them makes no sense (i.e. generates no new proposition), Russell thinks he can use his (admittedly problematic) way of defining propositions to define a proposition containing an asymmetrical relation. Russell is unhappy about several aspects of his analysis of these cases, especially the fact that it commits him to saying that molecular connectives belong in the proposition though not in the atomic complex, but he shrugs it off as inevitable, since we cannot explain differences in sense (e.g. 'a is before b' versus 'b is before a') in terms of elements and form alone.

29–30 May: 'Belief, Disbelief and Doubt'

I have been maintaining throughout this study that Russell is attempting to address Wittgenstein's point that judging must involve a proposition, which cannot be either a mere complex or something dependent on our mental states, and that at Wittgenstein's urging he is beginning to develop a conception of propositions as bi-polar, that is, such that p and $\sim p$ are complementary aspects of a single proposition. This view stems from Wittgenstein's insight that logical constants are not entities comprising a proposition but operations we make with a proposition. Instead of a separate entity added to a proposition, a proposition is either negated (asserting a fact) or negated again (asserting the opposite fact), but those are two possibilities intrinsic to the use of proposition and not objects either present or absent in it. As I have already suggested, when Russell tells Ottoline on the 24th of coming upon a 'new way' of arranging the material in his manuscript, he is referring to his decision not to divide the later parts of the manuscript between belief and inference (his original plan) but between atomic propositional acts of mind and molecular propositional acts of mind.[28] This decision shows, I think, that he has become persuaded that a proper account of judgement should show that something, a proposition, is significant apart from those contexts in which it is asserted or denied, and that it is logically prior to notions like 'not'. These themes belong to Wittgenstein's emerging conception of propositional bipolarity. Russell's discussion in his chapter on understanding speaks to the need for a proposition that contributes meaning to cognitive acts while remaining logically neutral, neither affirmative nor negative, but his analysis has to go further to capture the complementary or bipolar nature of a proposition, and to express this he introduces the notion of a propositional pair of relations, *believing* and *disbeliev-ing*, towards the same objects and relation.[29] Instead of taking the contradictory of the belief that, for example, lead is heavier than gold as the belief that gold is not heavier than lead, Russell defines the contradictory of the belief as the disbelief that gold is heavier than lead.

Russell's analysis raises numerous questions concerning his account of truth and falsehood. In particular, throughout *Theory of Knowledge* Russell characterizes falsehood in terms of the absence of a fact, though he also says 'it seems quite evident that the truth or falsehood of a belief depends on something purely objective'.[30] Assuming that his view in this chapter is still one that bases truth and falsehood on something objective, the question is, what sort of 'objective' thing has got to exist on his account? In later work Russell sometimes seems to say that a reduction of negative propositions to states of disbelief makes it appear as though the truth of, say, 'this is not hot' depends on the subjective event of experiencing disbelief, whereas a proposition must be true because of some fact even if that requires the acceptance of negative facts. In 1918 he argues for the existence of negative facts, while agreeing with Demos that:

> a negative proposition is in no way dependent on a cognitive subject for its definition . . . You have got to find something or other in the real world to make this disbelief true and the only question is what.[31]

It is unclear to me whether or not he holds this view in 1913 while writing his chapter on belief and disbelief. There is no evidence of Russell adopting negative facts in *Theory of Knowledge*, yet he must at least have reflected on the issue: it is impossible that Russell could have introduced the above analysis without seeing that it would bear on his account of what facts underlie the truth of a case of belief or disbelief. If he does accept the existence of negative facts, he is not being inconsistent with his claim that *and*, *or*, *not*, etc. are not genuine objects, for when, not long after writing this chapter, Russell does introduce a doctrine of negative facts (in notes), he denies that *not* occurs as an entity and claims that negative and positive facts are irreducibly different: no object or property makes a fact negative or positive. (In 1904 a similar idea is at work when Russell denies that negative propositions – or what makes them negative – can be perceived.) If his 1913 doctrine of belief and disbelief does assume the existence of negative facts, the need for them probably comes from considering the case of true disbelief. That is, Russell might conclude that the case of true disbelief requires the existence of negative facts because if what verifies a belief is the existence of a complex corresponding to the proposition believed, then what verifies a case of disbelief in that proposition can't also be the existence of that complex, and yet if what verifies one falsifies the other, what verifies disbelief can't be the absence of a fact, as that absence – i.e. nothing – would then ground the truth of the belief as well. Might Russell have reasoned in this or some similar way? Perhaps, but though I suspect that Russell intends a doctrine of negative facts in the current chapter, his surprisingly brief discussion leaves this question and other issues unanswered. His next chapter shows him addressing truth and falsehood – in fact, it shows him getting mired in the difficulties an account of truth presents his doctrine of propositions – but it adds little to answer the questions left open in the chapter on the belief/disbelief pair.

31 May–1 June: 'Truth and Falsehood'

Turning from belief and disbelief to truth and falsehood – which are properties of beliefs and propositions as opposed to sentences[32] – Russell defines a belief as *true* when 'there is a certain complex which must be a definable function of the belief, and which we shall call the *corresponding* complex, or the *corresponding fact*'.[33] Of course, when a belief is true, certain complexes may exist that do not correspond to it, but on Russell's definition, the truth of a belief requires the existence not just of any fact but a corresponding fact, and as it turns out, his theory of belief cannot demonstrate this for all cases of belief. That is, certain cases show that on his theory there is no essential connection between what a belief asserts (its *sense*, in Wittgenstein's jargon) and what makes it true. The arbitrary quality of the connection between truth and belief bears on the relation between judging and naming, since in demonstrating that to each true belief (and presumably each true disbelief) there corresponds a unique complex, he would succeed in demonstrating the existence of unique names that apply to the corresponding complexes. His failure to show that the belief and what makes it true are related essentially is therefore a failure to show that a judgement and a name for some complex correspond in anything more than an accidental way. Finally, his inability to use perception to pick out a unique complex illustrates the weakness in his perceptual foundation, while showing that he has no defence against scepticism and opening up an issue that takes on greater importance in the next two chapters.

The problem with his account of propositions or belief is not apparent immediately, for it seems to work in cases like 'A believes that a is similar to b'. Since a, b, *similarity* and the dual form xRy determine a unique complex, only this complex will exist and correspond to the belief when the belief is true. Indeed, we seem to be able to name that complex merely by joining together the simple names whose meanings are the individual items in the complex. But though Russell resists for a while longer, this case really only appears to work – to locate a corresponding complex – because in this case no other complex is possible; that is, the connection between the proposition and what makes it true is only accidental and not essential. Ironically, in this very chapter Russell dismisses the causal theory of James and the neutral monists on the grounds that they fail to establish an essential, non-arbitrary, connection between a belief and being called true.

The fact that Russell has failed to single out an essential connection between a belief and a complex or fact that verifies it becomes clear when he turns to beliefs that involve asymmetrical relations. Recall that Russell decides he can only disambiguate belief in an asymmetrical relation of terms (e.g. a-before-b) by analysing it by means of a new, closely associated complex (a-is-earlier-in-γ and b-is-later-in-γ).[34] This analysis flies in the face of our understanding of what it means to say a belief is true. Our intuitions about the meaning of 'true' tell us that even if a complex always and only exists when a belief is true, if it doesn't correspond to what a belief says or means, it is irrelevant: what makes a belief true has to be tied to what the belief says. This demand follows in part from recognizing that any number of complexes might coincide with the truth of a certain belief, but if what verifies a belief is a complex with no connection to the sense of proposition asserted by the belief, then which complex is the truth-making one strikes us as completely arbitrary.

Seeing this, Russell admits that his theory fails to analyse 'what we were already meaning by the "truth"', since by calling a judgement 'true' we mean that a fact verifies it, not that it corresponds to a further fact associated with that fact. Yet in saying this he is conceding only that there are difficulties in his doctrine of propositions in the case of asymmetrical relations; in these cases, truth 'may be said . . . [to be] arbitrary in our account'[35] in the sense that 'we might equally have taken any other complex as the one which must exist if our belief is to be true'.[36] He insists that his theory of belief works in some cases, since symmetric complexes are 'as intimately associated with our belief as anything purely objective can be'.[37] I suspect that this is optimistic; Wittgenstein's point, which is almost certainly reflected in this concern, is that though Russell's analysis of symmetrical relations seems protected against this kind of objection, it really isn't, and his account of asymmetrical relations merely exposes that his account of the relation of fact to belief is arbitrary.

Russell's failure to illustrate the intimate connection between what verifies a proposition and what it says is not the only difficulty recorded in this chapter. We just saw that his theory seems to give an arbitrary account of the connection between the belief fact and the complex that verifies it. It might seem that his doctrine of perception – the claim that we can perceive the unique complex that verifies a belief – protects him from this account. This possible defence is attacked, however, when Russell notes that 'it may be asked how truth and error can be distinguished if our account is correct'.[38] On his view, we know that a belief is true and not false when we have acquaintance with the corresponding complex. For example, we can determine the truth of the proposition 'X believes that A is similar to B' by means of acquaintance with the complex a-similar-b, and 'this will', he says, 'assure us of the truth of the belief that A and B are similar'.[39] Implied in the objection, though, is that the success of perception in this case is superficial and not essential; it only seems that perception takes us to a unique complex because in the case of symmetrical relations like *similarity*, it makes no difference whether we perceive a-similar-b or b-similar-a. But in other cases the difference we ignore in symmetrical cases will be pressing. Indeed, Russell's complicated analysis of asymmetrical relations is made necessary just because constituents and form alone do not in these cases determine a unique fact, and that is determined only by establishing the way they are combined. But if this is the case then we cannot trust perception to establish the truth of a belief in an asymmetrical relation, for we have no means other than perception to ascertain that the complex perceived *as we perceive it* is the one that corresponds to the belief in question. I noted above that Russell's remarks on perception in *Theory of Knowledge* point towards the kinds of considerations present in the *Tractatus* when Wittgenstein writes that in perceiving 'we really see two different facts'.[40] The possibility of seeing different facts implies that perception cannot ground truth even on those occasions where it appears to do so, that is, even in cases of belief asserting symmetrical relations like 'X believes that a is similar to b'. That is, if I have no other means than perception to determine whether the complex asserted in a belief corresponds to the data I perceive in the *way* I perceive it or to the same data perceived in some other way, then I can't use perception to determine whether the belief corresponds to the data as I see it and is true or fails to correspond to the data as I see it and is false.

Besides mentioning these problems, Russell also acknowledges the implications of his attempt to explicate belief in asymmetric relations in terms of conjunctions of propositions. In order to exist as a fact, the components of a belief must exist, and in this case those components will be atomic propositions. Yet if the belief is false, these components will be false, and since they must exist to comprise the belief itself, it follows that his analysis means that beliefs will 'contain false atomic propositions as constituents', that is, his account of asymmetrical relations implies 'the admission of false propositions in an objective sense'.[41] Though this is a serious problem, Russell turns quickly to another rising objection, that 'there must be non-mental propositions as opposed to complexes, and that therefore beliefs had better be interpreted as dealing with propositions'.[42] Of course, he is in the midst of defending a doctrine of objective propositions and has been since a few days before his most recent meeting with Wittgenstein on the 26th. This objection (which along with the others in this chapter may reflect Wittgenstein's comments on the 26th) therefore appears to dismiss his doctrine of propositions and to insist on treating beliefs as about propositions, that is, vehicles of sense, rather than as about complexes. In other words, it draws our attention to the need to distinguish the fact of believing, which involves entities of some kind, from what the belief says, the proposition or sense – a point Wittgenstein makes in his 'Notes on Logic' when he says that in 'A believes *p*' A is not in a relation to a complex. Russell takes this objection as a demand for the sort of objective entities from which he has freed himself:

> [T]he admission of such entities – which must be capable of falsehood as well as truth – runs counter to the rejection of unrealities . . . which seems to me . . . necessary . . . to all sound philosophy.[43]

2–6 May: Self-Evidence

When Russell turns to the question of the nature of self-evident judgements, some of the issues involved in the last chapter on truth reappear, such as his failure to establish a correspondence between judgements and facts that is sufficiently intimate. In the present chapter he defines the truth of self-evident judgements, as he does in *Principia*, in terms of the perception of complexes, and this raises problems not unlike the ones I have argued are implicit in his chapter on truth.

After pointing out what we mean by the word 'knowledge' – it can't consist of true beliefs whose truth is known fortuitously or by inference from other beliefs or with some lingering doubt – Russell defends the existence of self-evident judgements by considering what the possibility of knowledge requires us to infer about judgement. For knowledge to exist, the truth of our beliefs – or at least the truth of some of them – must be resistant to doubt, and this 'resistance and stability', he says, rests, 'in the last resort, upon self-evidence'.[44] That is, if any genuine knowledge is possible, then 'there must be knowledge, independent of inference'.[45] That is, there must be 'a class of beliefs which can be known to be true'.[46] Though self-evident beliefs must therefore actually be true, Russell can't use the concept of *truth* to define the class of self-evident beliefs since he intends to use the set of self-evident beliefs to define how we use the word 'true'.

What, then, is the characteristic by which we recognize self-evident beliefs? Russell's own view – presented in the *Principia*, the *Problems of Philosophy* and elsewhere – is that a judgement is self-evident 'when it is contemporaneous with acquaintance with the corresponding complex'.[47] For example, the judgement that the sun is shining is self-evident when we are able to perceive the complex, the-shining-sun. To say that '*b* is evident', on this view, is to say '*b* is simultaneous with perception of the corresponding complex'.[48] But there are problems with this definition. The objection that Russell's account of the correspondence of belief and fact is too external is familiar. It isn't enough to call a judgement is self-evident 'when it is contemporaneous with acquaintance with the corresponding complex',[49] for on that definition simply perceiving a complex justifies calling the corresponding judgement self-evident even when we don't perceive that the two correspond, and surely it is essential to what we mean by calling a judgement self-evident that we know that it corresponds to a complex we perceive.[50] In short, self-evidence can't be secured by acquaintance with any complex or even the corresponding complex, nor is it sufficient to require simultaneity of the perception and the complex; put in any of these ways, self-evidence appears to be 'altogether too extraneous' as a property of judgements. To explain self-evident belief, he decides we must perceive the correspondence between the judgement and the complex, for the 'relevance of the complex to the judgement must also be given in experience, otherwise the two fall apart'.[51]

Yet perception of the correspondence is problematic in the case of judgements of perception, i.e. analytic judgements like 'a is part of the complex aRb'. On his definition of self-evidence, 'a is part of the complex aRb' is self-evident if we perceive and grasp the relevance of its correspondence to the complex from which the judgement emerges, namely, a-part-of-aRb. By adding the additional constraints, he seems to require us to make another judgement, that this judgement corresponds to this perceived complex, and since this new judgement ought to be self-evident as well, his view,

> though perhaps not definitely refutable, makes analysis very complicated, and introduces great difficulties into the theory of the correspondence which defines truth.[52]

Despite these objections, Russell decides that, on balance, there are sufficient reasons for preferring his doctrine to the alternatives, for example the inductive argument that our knowledge reduces to probabilities, the Idealist argument that reasoning is ultimately circular and the sceptic's denial of genuine knowledge. His discussion of scepticism is particularly interesting in light of his earlier conversations with Wittgenstein and because of some of the problems facing his multiple relation theory of judgement. As Russell describes it, the sceptic is one who adopts the habit of 'complete abstinence from belief'.[53] Because of this 'the sceptical philosophy is brief; it begins and ends in questioning. By nature, it cannot argue, or seek to establish any result, even its own tenability.'[54] Because 'argument ceases and refutation is impossible' with regard to scepticism, Russell's response to the sceptic is simply to point out that the desire to go beyond questions reasserts itself, and that a non-sceptical philosophy 'claims a longer attention' than does that species of philosophy engaging in it as 'fundamentally a questioning attitude'.[55]

If we see Wittgenstein as questioning the sort of philosophical attitude that issues into statements of theory and beliefs or doctrines, then Russell's comments here are particularly ironic, for they occur as he is attempting to come to grips with Wittgenstein's objections, and yet he does not seem to sense that Wittgenstein is committed to a conception of philosophy quite opposed to his own pursuit of philosophical theories and doctrines. Wittgenstein's movement towards a conception of philosophy as 'an activity, not a doctrine' is probably well under way at this time. Indeed, Russell's identification of the 'questioning attitude' of the sceptic with a view of life as one involving 'undisciplined impulse'[56] is perhaps behind his earlier report to Ottoline that Wittgenstein 'abominates ethics and morals generally; he is deliberately a creature of impulse, and thinks one should be'.[57] But if this is Wittgenstein's way of conveying his estrangement from Russell's doctrinal style of philosophy, Russell seems not to have noticed.

In this chapter Russell dismisses scepticism on practical grounds, but earlier in the manuscript he uses our knowledge of certain types of propositions to show that his doctrine of acquaintance doesn't collapse into solipsism, and it is interesting to wonder why he doesn't introduce a similar argument here against scepticism. Briefly, in defending his mind/matter dualism against attack from various quarters (e.g. neutral monism), he considers the objection that his doctrine of acquaintance seems to make 'the experience of each moment . . . a prison for the knowledge of the moment, . . . as though its boundaries must be the boundaries of our present world'.[58] If he cannot show how knowledge is possible beyond that given in the present moment, then his doctrine of acquaintance will collapse into solipsism, the view that my total experience is all embracing, and that nothing can be known beyond what I experience in the present instant. Though no final refutation can be given to the solipsist, Russell thinks that it is possible to give a partial refutation based on the fact that 'we may know propositions of the form "there are things having such and such a property", even when we do not know any instance of such things'.[59] For example, despite the fact that in the sequence of all the prime numbers we will ever live to think, there is a greatest, we know there is no greatest prime number. Hence mathematics provides knowledge that exceeds the boundary of present experience. But mundane examples can also be provided; for example, knowing that there is a thing, 'the father of Jones' solely by knowing Jones, *paternity*, and the fact that every man has a father. Here too we have descriptive knowledge that exceeds the boundaries of our present experience. It is thus his theory of descriptions and judgement involving those descriptions that protects his doctrine of acquaintance from the charge of solipsism and scepticism, for from the existence of such propositions it follows that 'what is experienced at any moment is known not to be the sum total of the things in the world'.[60] Why does Russell not use this argument in the present chapter? We've already seen that he has difficulty explaining propositions like 'there are things having such and such a relation' when no such relation occurs, and that his account of propositions, by deriving them from facts of understanding, seems to require that there exist an instance of things in that relation. It is possible that doubts arising from his recent struggles with the form of such propositions lead Russell to avoid making a similar argument here against scepticism. Even if this is not the case, the connection between his theory of propositions and his defence against solipsism is worth noting, for flaws in his conception of the proposition amount to weaknesses in one line of defence against solipsism.

6–7 May: Degrees of Certainty

Having shown the possibility of knowledge to be grounded in self-evident judgements that are derived from indubitable experiences, Russell turns to the related question anything in the nature or constituents of a belief that might make it more or less certain than another belief. His question is not a psychological one so much as an ontological one about whether some beliefs are inherently more or less certain than others, i.e. whether 'there is any ground for believing some things more firmly than others'.[61] Additional tasks are to show that there is a way of deciding what level of certainty a belief possesses and to show that there is a way of choosing between competing beliefs. As might be expected given his previous chapter, certainty characterizes beliefs located at the juncture between perception of a complex and the corresponding judgement, and for the most part, the topic of the chapter is whether any beliefs are such that they are intrinsically uncertain, such as beliefs based on certain kinds of memory of past objects. In the chapter as a whole Russell does not address the concerns pressed on him by Wittgenstein, and the details of his discussion in this chapter can be omitted.

Part one, on atomic thought, comes to a close with Russell's chapter on certainty. In the remainder of the chapter Russell summarizes his analysis of atomic thought in preparation for a transition to a discussion of molecular thought. On 6 June Russell finishes the chapter on certainty. He reports this fact to Lady Ottoline the following day and tells her he will return to it soon. On 8 June he tells Lady Ottoline he won't try to finish the analytic section yet (concerning descriptions and molecular thought) but will take a holiday.

Conclusion

To what did Wittgenstein violently react, when Russell showed him part of the chapter on understanding? I have already touched on some aspects of these remarks, namely, that what Wittgenstein had tried and knew wouldn't work was the attempt to introduce a complex to preserve types, since the type difference between a complex and a term is lost, in so far as they are both treated as objects. But, I think, there is probably a great deal more to Wittgenstein's claim that Russell's attempt is 'all wrong'. I suggested above that Wittgenstein's objection on the 20th concerns in part Russell's belief that judgement is a grouping of objects – a complex of objects – related to a thinking subject. Russell's attempt on the 26th to arrive at the 'proposition' as more than a merely fictional subjective element – that is, his emphasis on the need to find some common element – is, I think, a response to Wittgenstein's noting that sense, a proposition, must exist prior to affirming, negating and other mental acts. In stressing this, Wittgenstein is rejecting Russell's tendency to conflate what occurs in the symbol with what occurs in the judgement or proposition as a complex or fact, that is, as a relation among objects. Russell's attempt to give a *map* of the relations holding among propositional constituents shows explicitly that he makes this mistake; he tries to depict a proposition by lines drawn in space. In addition, it is likely that part of Wittgenstein's objection was to the inclusion of form, for if the form occurs as a simple it can't do the job of uniting it is supposed to be able to do, but if it occurs as a complex, it amounts to a rule on whose basis a proposition is a unity and makes sense. But a rule cannot determine that a proposition must make sense, as sense is presupposed by the rule. The inclusion of form in Russell's analysis is questionable in another way as well, for the subject either does or does not actually relate the items judged to the form, but if they are related, then the judgement is true (and it must be possible for it not to be), but if they are not related by means of the form – if the relation among the items does not occur – then the proposition loses its integrity as a vehicle of sense.

The difficulties that arise from Russell's conception of judgement as a species of fact are not confined to the role of the relation, and in the preceding pages I have discussed tensions within Russell's account of analysis and truth, as well as suggestions of difficulties within his theory of self-evidence. In the following chapter I turn to notes Russell writes in this period, and in these notes many of these problems reappear.

Chapter 4

The Form of Belief

[A]s soon as we reach the theory of judgement, even apart from truth and falsehood, the difficulties encountered are almost entirely logical, and logical discoveries are what are most required for the progress of the subject.[1]

Introduction

In this study as a whole I have been asking: how does Wittgenstein have an impact on the development of Russell's ideas during his writing of the text, and how are signs of that impact evident in the text itself? Though I have also been driving towards the answer to another question – why did Russell abandon the *Theory of Knowledge*? – giving a direct answer to that question has not been possible until this chapter. In turning to it now, to the reasons for the demise of the manuscript, it is important to recall Russell's remarks about Wittgenstein's criticisms. In 1916 he writes to Ottoline that Wittgenstein persuaded him that he couldn't do foundational work in logic, and by that he means the analysis of forms. On 28 May 1913 he writes to Ottoline that Wittgenstein's 'criticisms have to do with the problems I want to leave to him – which makes a complication',[2] and on 1 June he tells Ottoline that his difficulties are bound up with the 'difficulty of not stealing [Wittgenstein's] ideas'.[3] In the following I argue that by 'Wittgenstein's ideas' Russell means Wittgenstein's analysis of the form of proposition as essentially bipolar and directed either towards or away from a fact. I further argue that Russell agrees with Wittgenstein on this point and that his difficulties come from his attempt to explain the form of a proposition in such a way that it isn't a name for a fact but stands to it in two relations. That is, I believe the core problem leading to the demise of the book to be

Russell's inability to explain propositional bipolarity within the framework of his theory of judgement.

My explanation of why Wittgenstein's objections to Russell's bungled account of bipolarity cause Russell to abandon the manuscript also takes into account the fact that even though he can go no further on the manuscript, Russell doesn't abandon his theory of judgement.[4] In 1917, for example, he says that Wittgenstein persuaded him that his theory is 'somewhat unduly simple', and he seems to think that the theory only needs a 'modification'. In addition, in many other places in the period between 1913 and 1918 he refers to judgement as a multiple relation, that is, a fact, albeit a puzzling one with a form unlike other forms of facts. Given this, my question becomes not, why did Russell abandon the *Theory of Knowledge*?, but what about his attempt to do justice to the bipolarity of a proposition that leads him to abandon the *Theory of Knowledge* and yet doesn't lead him to reject his theory of judgement? That is, what kind of attack might Wittgenstein have made sufficient to cause Russell to abandon the text while continuing for some time to have faith in his theory of judgement?

A partial answer to this question comes from looking at notes in Russell's hand covering some three pages and titled 'Props'.[5] Based on their content, the editors argue that the notes appear 'to be an attempt to take account of Wittgenstein's new theory of propositions'.[6] These notes show very clearly what difficulties Russell faces – in particular, the status of the relation in the belief fact and the difficulty of giving a non-arbitrary account of the correspondence of belief to fact. The diagrams in the notes are considered in a later section of the present chapter and show, I think, that Russell sees that the form of belief cannot be represented spatially – i.e. is not explicable in terms of a complex – and that it falls outside of the series of atomic and molecular forms.

Before turning to the notes, a word about their date of origin: some evidence indicates that the notes were written during or shortly after the third week of May. For example, Russell composed and then rejected a page of text concerning Meinong in the third week of May, and the first page of 'Props' occurs on the back of that page. The editors of *Theory of Knowledge* hesitate to assert that 'Props' dates from the third week of May, on the grounds that we do not know that Wittgenstein's thought so clearly represented in it was as advanced as this would indicate.[7] Yet the notes are perhaps evidence that it was; after all, Russell was not in the habit of keeping such pages around for long periods of time, and the material in the notes overlaps so much with the concerns Russell raises in later chapters of *Theory of Knowledge* that Blackwell, speaking on his own behalf, judges them to originate in May, 'very soon after Wittgenstein's second visit', that is, sometime shortly after the 26th of May.[8] There is good reason for this view: the notes reject the theory that occurs in Russell's chapter on understanding propositions, and that suggests that they were composed shortly after Wittgenstein's third, angry, visit, that is, on or shortly after May 26th.

'Prop[osition]s'

In Chapter 2 of this study I argued that in the *Theory of Knowledge* Russell tries to provide what Wittgenstein is pressing for – something prior to assertion and denial – by treating understanding as a logically neutral act of mind. But his attempt fails to get the essential thing, that a proposition or sense must be bipolar, relevant either to a negative fact or a positive one, independently of being asserted or denied. In these notes he revisits the nature of the proposition, moving much closer to Wittgenstein's views. Yet his account does not break away from the epistemological framework even though it changes some aspects of it. For example, in *Theory of Knowledge* Russell took understanding to be a multiple relation (except in certain special cases), and in these notes it appears to be a direct cognitive relation to a complex; at the same time the notion of understanding is here allied if not identified with that of perception.[9] (A diagram accompanying his discussion shows this plainly and is discussed in the next section.) Moreover Russell attempts to use the resources of his realist and atomist theory of meaning to explain the connection between a proposition and its sense, that is, its two truth possibilities. Understanding is therefore explained in terms of our grasp on something in the world.

He opens the notes by stating that there are two kinds of complex, negative and positive:

Three objects *x*, *R*, *y* form one or other of two complexes xRy or ~xRy.

These negative and positive facts, as he thereafter calls them, are said to 'contain nothing but *x* and *R* and *y*'; that is, despite the suggestion of the symbol '~xRy', a negative fact contains no object corresponding to the tilde. Shifting to the nature of the proposition and of understanding, Russell argues that the proposition 'points indifferently' to either fact, and that in understanding a proposition xRy what occurs 'points equally to either of these two complexes – at least it points to whichever there is of these two'.[10] Earlier we saw Russell struggle to explain how we can understand a proposition in the absence of perception of a confirming complex and when the belief is false; here, instead of positing form as what we understand, he finds something in the world, something in which a relation occurs as a relation, as the thing that we grasp when we understand a proposition:

It *looks* as if there actually were always a relation of x and R and y whenever they form *either* of the two complexes, and as if this were perceived in understanding. If there is such a neutral fact, it ought to be a *constituent* of the positive or negative fact. It will provide a meaning for *possibility*.[11]

These notes tell us that when we understand, there is something, a fact, and it is this that we perceive and understand. The fact we understand is not the negative or positive one, however, though it is associated with them because it is in some sense contained in them.[12] What happens in understanding a proposition is that we perceive some logically neutral fact that exists whenever either the relevant positive or a negative fact exists. For example, if our complex a-is-left-of-b, Russell's point is that some relation of a, b, and *left of* must exist whether a is to the left of b or a is not to the left of b, and his further point is that what we grasp when we understand a proposition is one disjunct of the disjunction of possibilities aLb v ~aLb.

Moving from understanding to judging, Russell makes the neutral fact a constituent of judging, replacing form:

> Judgement involves the *neutral* fact, not the positive or negative fact . . . The neutral fact replaces the *form.*[13]

As we saw, in the *Theory of Knowledge* Russell hopes to use form either as an explicit component of judging or in some less pronounced way to explain the content or unity of a judgement in the case where a complex might not exist or is not given in experience. Russell wrote, then, that:

> In an actual complex, the general form is not presupposed; but when we are concerned with a proposition which may be false, and where, therefore, the actual complex is not given, . . . the general form of the merely supposed complex should be given.[14]

He has now apparently come to believe that his doctrine of form can not do the work it's supposed to do, for in a belief the subordinate relation must occur as a relation, not as a term held up for comparison with a template or form. For in the notes form is replaced by a neutral fact; and since in such facts a relation occurs as such, the result is that an actual complex always is 'given' in an act of understanding.

The neutral fact, which differs from form in being a genuine constituent of (either a negative or a positive) fact, serves as the content of judging, and, in being judged, corresponds either to a negative or a positive fact. The passage cited above reads in full:

> Judgement involves the *neutral* fact, not the positive or negative fact. The neutral fact has a relation to a positive fact, or to a negative fact. Judgement asserts *one* of these. It will still be a neutral relation, but its terms will not be the same as in my old theory. The neutral fact replaces the *form.*[15]

In the citation above Russell distinguishes between what judging *involves* and what it *asserts*, anticipating his later distinction, late in 1918 and in the early 1920s, between what a judgement expresses and what it denotes, but without yet associating these notions with a doctrine of the mental versus the objective domain.[16] By claiming that a judgement 'involves' a neutral relation or fact Russell evidently wishes to explain how a judgement has content when the relation it asserts doesn't hold, i.e. when the judgement is false. At the same time, Russell begins moving closer to the idea he expresses in 1922 when he credits Wittgenstein with the idea that 'the objective reference is not determined by the fact alone, but by the direction of the belief towards or away from the fact'.[17] This is evident in the notes when he writes:

> Call neutral fact 'positively directed' when it corresponds to a positive fact, 'negatively directed' when it corresponds to a negative fact.[18]

He then lays down the relation between negative and positive facts and between the corresponding judgement pair:

> The negative of the positive or negative fact is the negative or positive fact. There is no negative of the neutral proposition or of the neutral fact. Call +J(xRy) the judgement *of* +xRy, etc. Then the negative of a judgement is the judgement *of* the negative.[19]

Reasoning that assertion and negation must characterize the act not the constituents of judging, Russell prefixes the signs for assertion and negation to the relation of judging, symbolizing belief that xRy as +J(xRy) and disbelief that xRy as –J(xRy).[20] Thus in *Theory of Knowledge* '~aRb' is defined as disbelief that aRb. Going beyond his discussion of belief, disbelief and truth in *Theory of Knowledge*, when he addresses the correspondence of belief to fact, he includes the case of negative judgements. A judgement, he suggests, corresponds to a fact when the affirmative or negative quality of the judging matches the affirmative or negative quality of the fact, and when the constituents of the neutral fact involved in judging are the same as the constituents of the positive or negative fact. That is:

> The correspondence in judgement is between +J(xRy) and +(xRy) and –J(xRy) and (xRy) and ±J(xRy) and ± (xRy).[21]

I noted above that a neutral fact, which forms the content or meaning of the belief, is associated with the (negative or positive) fact that makes the belief true. The tactic of bringing in associated facts or complexes to explain the relationship between what a proposition says and what makes it true is problematic in several respects, and it is not surprising that immediately after the above remarks, Russell concludes the notes with the following worries:

> This correspondence, however, entails the old difficulties: it seems not intimate enough. And it suggests dangers of an infinite regress. It can't be quite right. There will only be a neutral fact when the objects are of the right types. This introduces great difficulties.[22]

We have already seen some of these 'old difficulties'. In the *Theory of Knowledge* Russell admits that on his theory of propositions there is no essential connection between the proposition and the fact that verifies it, and even if only one fact exists to do the job of verifying, the connection is still arbitrary.[23] At that juncture the problem seemed to him to concern only propositions asserting asymmetrical relations; here he is seeing that the same sort of problem occurs with respect to distinguishing positive and negative propositions. For the existence of a fact that verifies a belief (or disbelief) isn't enough: our intuitions about the meaning of the word 'true' tell us that what makes a judgement true must be uniquely tied to what the judgement says, and it will be completely arbitrary which other fact we select as truth-maker among those that happen to exist when the judgement is true. Because the neutral fact is not the same as the fact that verifies the judgement it amounts to much the same role and causes much the same problem as his 'associated complex' did in his analysis of asymmetrical relations. That is, it causes what

Russell alludes to as the 'lack of intimacy' in his account of the correspondence between judgements and facts.

Moreover, to clarify their connection, to emphasize the intimacy of the correspondence between a belief and a fact, requires another judgement, and in that judgement the same problem reappears.[24] Russell thus worries that his account 'suggests dangers of an infinite regress' and 'can't be quite right'.[25] Moreover, in these notes a neutral fact replaces form: it serves the purpose of providing what it is we understand, a content in which the items occur as united or related. Thus like form, the neutral fact comprising the judgement fact and associated with the negative or positive fact serves as a premise that the ingredients of the judgement are united into a whole. As Wittgenstein will soon point out, the integrity of a proposition, its existence as a proposition or vehicle of sense, cannot depend on a further proposition, for that presupposes that propositions possess sense, hence sense must be somehow built in.

Notice that the neutral fact, unlike the form it replaces, is a complex not a simple. When Russell says, 'There will only be a neutral fact when the objects are of the right types', he is acknowledging that in the neutral fact the relation (which is the subordinate relation of the judgement) has to occur as a relation not as a term. As I noted in Chapter 1, Wittgenstein's objection on the 20th – and probably throughout this period – concerns Russell's attempt to bridge the way in which a relation occurs in a fact of believing with that in which it occurs in a proposition. In these notes Russell is using the neutral fact in a way that attempts to bridge how a relation occurs in a fact with how it occurs in a vehicle of sense, but doing so only causes difficulties. In particular, if the subordinate relation in the neutral fact doesn't occur as a relation, the belief has no content ('involves' nothing), but if it does hold and relate items, and the fact the judgement asserts by means of it is false, then there is no correspondence between what the judgement says or involves (a neutral fact in which a relation holds between objects) and the fact that falsifies it (in which no such relation holds). The general problem is one he will address later in terms of the belief fact containing two verbs. In his 1918 lectures on logical atomism, Russell emphasizes that in judging 'there are two verbs at least' and that it is impossible to put the subordinate verb 'on a level with its terms as an object term in the belief'.[26] He adds:

That is a point in which I think that the theory of judgement which I set forth once in print some years ago was a little unduly simple, because I then did treat the object verb as if one could put it as just an object like the terms, as if one could put 'loves' on a level with Desdemona and Cassio as a term for the relation 'believe'.[27]

These notes suggest that what contributes to Russell's decision to put aside work on *Theory of Knowledge* is his inability to explain the form of belief in a way that captures propositional bipolarity and the essential connection between the proposition's sense and the fact that verifies it. A central problem in his inability to do so is his ongoing conception of the proposition as a complex containing a relation, or rather two relations, but while he does not break free of this conception in the notes, examining his use of various diagrams in 'Props' shows that he is beginning to be aware of the problem and to conceive of belief as in a form of fact wholly unlike others, and it is in turning to this issue that, I suggest, we see why he abandons the *Theory of Knowledge* text and not the theory of judgement.

The Diagrams in 'Props'

In his 1918 lectures on logical atomism Russell alludes to problems with a theory of symbolism, having already noted that it is impossible to draw a 'map-in-space' or diagram of the form of belief.[28] Two diagrams occurring in Russell's work in 'Props' anticipate his 1918 discussion of the problems of symbolizing belief. These sketches clearly show Russell struggling to accommodate his own view of belief to Wittgenstein's conception of propositions. The first sketch concerns understanding. As we have already seen, Russell explains *understanding* in these notes in terms of direct perception of a fact. Since we can't perceive negative facts, perception can take place in one way only: as directed towards positive facts.

Figure 5. *Diagram in 'Props' of understanding*[29]

In his illustration of understanding in Figure 5, a proposition of the form xRy points directly to a fact relating x and y. Note that the proposition contains as a term what occurs in the fact as a relation between terms, indicated by an arrow. As noted above, Russell's diagram presents understanding in a way strikingly at odds with his view in the *Theory of Knowledge*. There, however simple it is – abstract or logically neutral – compared to other cognitive acts, the mental relation *understanding* is unequivocally a multiple relation holding between a subject and the various objects comprising her understanding. Here *understanding* is depicted as a dual relation. In fact, in these notes it is difficult to see how *understanding* differs from simple perception, except that the act of mind is depicted as involving the form of a proposition xRy.

The depiction of judging shown in Figure 6 is also strikingly different from his diagrams of judgement in the *Theory of Knowledge*. In the new sketch he abstracts entirely from the content of belief and shows what is essential to judging to be its bipolarity, indicated at the top of the sketch by the combined +/– signs. The sketch depicts judging as potentially corresponding to either a negative or a positive fact; that is, a broken line, common to the two cases, indicates that it is possible for a judgement to possess the opposite polarity and mean the opposite kind of fact.

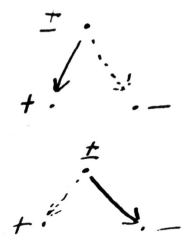

Figure 6. *Diagram in 'Props' of the bipolarity of judging* [30]

Wittgenstein surely influences Russell's diagram, and for the sake of contrast Wittgenstein's diagram of bipolarity in the *Notes on Logic* appears in Figure 7.

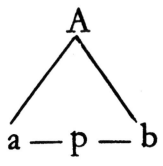

Figure 7. *Wittgenstein's diagram in* Notes on Logic *of the poles of a proposition* [31]

The point is not the superficial resemblance – a shared shape – but the point being made in each case. In Figures 6 and 7 what is being shown is that a proposition is essentially bipolar, that is, its sense is prior to being asserted or denied (independent of logical constants), and is therefore such that it can be either asserted or denied. At the same time, these diagrams show how the sense of proposition, as something prior to depiction, implies the conditions under which it is true and therefore under which it is false. For by the sign '$-p-$', Wittgenstein shows that the proposition's sense essentially contains or possesses the conditions under which it is true and the conditions under which it is false. As remarked in the introduction, Wittgenstein appears intent on persuading Russell to adopt an extensionalist account of proposition's meaning: here the identification of meaning with truth-conditions is explicit. Wittgenstein's diagram, like Russell's own, captures much the same point Russell expresses in 1918 with arrows pointing towards or away from a fact. For the sake of comparison that diagram occurs in Figure 8.

True: $\overrightarrow{\text{Prop.}}$ Fact

False: Fact $\overrightarrow{\text{Prop.}}$

Figure 8. *Russell's 1918 diagram of bipolarity*[32]

Russell's diagram of bipolarity expresses more information than his 1918 depiction – *viz.* that a proposition is positive or negative – but like the later one, and like Wittgenstein's, it attempts to show under what conditions a proposition is true and under what conditions false. I take the presence of the diagram in 'Props' to suggest that Russell is beginning to understood Wittgenstein's point.

Consider the difference between these illustrations and any of the ones considered in Chapter 2. As I already observed, the diagram used in the *Theory of Knowledge* and the diagrams leading up to it are spatial illustrations of the constituents and relations among constituents of a judging fact. That sensibility is absent from the sketch in Figures 6–8. These diagrams are intended to show the logical, not the spatial relation among the terms in the complex of judging. In the present case, no constituents at all appear in Russell's illustration of judging. Russell has bypassed a map – as he later calls it – of the form of a belief fact for a picture of its correspondence to fact. At the same time he adopts bipolarity, Russell is evidently taking the additional step of jettisoning the assumption that it is possible to make a map in space of belief, as nothing in space is of the same form as belief.

Most striking, however, is the absence of the subject from these two new cases (his diagram of the form of perception also leaves it out). In fact, at no place in 'Props' does Russell mention or depict the subject. I noted earlier that Russell thinks his 1913 theory of judgement is secured from neutral monist attack even without the subject as an object of introspected acquaintance. But as we also saw, this didn't prevent him from including the subject in his depictions of judgement and from talking about it.

If Russell's changed perspective is suggested by his neglecting to diagram the structure of belief, it is supported even more by his willingness to adopt a doctrine of propositional bipolarity. In doing so he appears to concede that a judging subject stands in no relation to a proposition's truth conditions or 'poles', but that these truth conditions are essential to the analysis of judgement. Occurring as and where they do – in the context of adopting a doctrine of propositions as bipolar – Russell's omissions are telling, and the notes in general show Russell in the process of conceding that propositions are bipolar, that no ordinary relation holds between a subject and the propositions' twin possibilities, and that spatial properties of a map or symbolism fail to capture the form of belief – all at the same time. Several months after Russell shelves his manuscript, Wittgenstein argues that the relation of the subject to the two poles of a proposition is 'not a relation in the ordinary sense'.[33] At that time the sketch shown above in Figure 7 is used to illustrate his point.

In his 1918 lectures on logical atomism Russell rejects the idea that the form of belief is that of a relation between a person and a proposition, even though certain ways of speaking like 'I believe the proposition p' and 'I believe that such and such' seem to suggest otherwise. Belief cannot be a relation to a fact, he notes, because there are no false facts. He argues further that in a belief proposition such as Othello's belief that Desdemona loves Cassio, *loves* must occur as a relation and can't be replaced by a substantive. Any map or diagram of belief will invariably depict the relation as existing, even when the belief is false, and will thus fail to capture the form of belief.

The Form of Belief

It is important to remember that Russell gives up on the *Theory of Knowledge* before he hears Wittgenstein's exact objection, and as I have noted already, he does so *without* giving up on his theory of judgement. The June letter is therefore not the cause of the demise of the book, though it certainly drives the last nail into the coffin. I have already suggested how the June letter bears on Russell's problems: when he reads it and speaks to Wittgenstein he will only be rehearsing what he's already concluded, that his account of the proposition and of judgement explains the proposition's sense in a way that is too external to the proposition, launching a regress and never explaining how the sense of a proposition 'aRb' implies 'aRb v ~aRb'. I turn in a moment to some other interpretations of the June letter, but before doing so I address the question, raised above: why Russell gives up the manuscript and not the theory of judgement.

In a portion of *Theory of Knowledge* revised and published after Wittgenstein's objections led to the demise of the text, Russell credits the 'unpublished work of my friend Mr. Ludwig Wittgenstein' for showing that 'all thought whose expression involves *propositions*, must be a fact of a different logical form from any of the series: subject–predicate facts, dual relations, triple relations, etc.'.[34] This is rather astonishing, considering that Wittgenstein seems intent on eliminating belief as a logical form. Moreover, Russell takes this new form to mean that:

> a difficult and interesting problem of pure logic arises, namely, the problem of enlarging the inventory of logical forms so as to include forms appropriate to the facts of epistemology.[35]

So by interpreting Wittgenstein's attack on judgement as an indication that belief is a new form of fact Russell takes from the one most opposed to blurring the line between logic and epistemology the need to do just that. Russell infers that the study of belief may fall *more* within philosophical logic than he had previously thought, i.e. a greater part of epistemology than he previously thought may fall within logic.

It would seem, therefore, that it is impossible to assign to the theory of knowledge a province distinct from that of logic and psychology.[36]

Though he attributes to Wittgenstein the discovery of a new form of fact, Russell is actually taking a position against Wittgenstein. Wittgenstein's conception of the nature of the proposition is one on which, as he later says, 'if a proposition is given, then all results of operations on it is given too, the construction of logic out of its signs must be clear'.[37] It is part of this view that we could completely describe the world in terms of the truth and falsity of all possible atomic propositions. But this view is only plausible if we eliminate beliefs. This point is made in the 1914 *Our Knowledge of the External World*. The question of what can be inferred from an atomic fact is connected to self-evidence; that is, Russell believes that some facts must be such that they cannot be inferred from other facts, but must simply be given. He writes:

Whether an atomic proposition, such as 'this is red', or 'this is before that' is to be asserted or denied can only be known empirically . . . It follows that, if atomic facts are to be known at all, some at least must be known without inference. The atomic facts which we come to know this way are the facts of sense-perception . . . If we knew all atomic facts, and also knew that there were none except those we knew, we should, theoretically, be able to infer truths of whatever form.[38]

He then adds the following note:

This perhaps requires modification in order to include such facts as beliefs and wishes, since such facts apparently contain propositions as components. Such facts, though not strictly atomic, must be supposed included if the statement in the text is to be true.[39]

The same insistence on belief facts occurs in Russell's notes to his copy of Wittgenstein's 'Notes on Logic'. As McGuinness points out:

[O]n f. 16, after 'If we formed all possible atomic propositions, the world will be completely described if we declared the truth or falsehood of each', there is added '[I doubt this]' . . . Clearly Russell is expressing a doubt about Wittgenstein's view: and we do indeed find the *view* expressed later in *Tractatus* 4.26 and the *doubt* in *Our Knowledge of the External World.*[40]

When Russell finally does give up the multiple relation theory of judgement in late 1918 he does so in the context of setting aside mind/matter dualism and rethinking a great deal of his philosophical assumptions.[41] At that time Wittgenstein's objections play a role – they give him incentive to find a new view – but they are by then not his only reasons for abandoning the theory, and many other factors play a role as well, such as coming to believe that his old arguments against neutral monism were invalid and based on a 'unnoticed bias'.[42] In 1913 this development has not yet taken place, and Russell can therefore see no good reason to deny subjective mental states, nor is there any good reason (since needing a way out of a jam is not a good reason) to eliminate beliefs. Because he has no ready analysis of the form of belief that will accommodate bipolarity and respond to Wittgenstein's objections but he at the same time can't fathom eliminating belief altogether, there is nothing left to do but stop, while professing that 'nothing that occurs in space is of the same form as belief'. 'The discovery of this fact', he says, 'is due to Mr. Wittgenstein.'[43]

The June Letter

Russell has already put aside the *Theory of Knowledge* text (on 8 June) and taken a week's holiday. When he returns in mid-June he receives a letter from Wittgenstein saying that he can now express 'exactly' his objection to Russell's theory of judgement. (By using the word 'exactly' Wittgenstein may be alluding to Russell's complaint that Wittgenstein was 'very inarticulate' in conversation on 26 May.)[44] What is the objection? '[I]t is obvious', according to Wittgenstein, that from the prop[osition] 'A judges that (say) a is in the Rel[ation] R to b', if correctly analysed, the prop[osition] 'aRb .v. ~aRb' must follow directly *without the use of any other premises*. This condition is not fulfilled by your theory.[45]

Despite its 'exactness', the nature of Wittgenstein's objection has been variously interpreted. Numerous authors have offered interpretations, and it is not my aim here to survey them in detail.[46] Some points ought, however, to be mentioned. First, Wittgenstein's objection seems to focus directly on Russell's attempt to explain propositions in terms of his doctrine of judgements, for when Wittgenstein expresses his regret to hear of Russell's 'paralysis' in light of the objection to his theory of judgement, he writes that only 'a correct theory of propositions' can remove it.[47] Second, there is general consensus that to require 'aRb v ~aRb' to follow from 'A judges that aRb' without another premise is equivalent to requiring that A judge a significant proposition. In *Principia*, Russell identifies *significance* with expressing a true or false proposition; thus a judgement is significant when either it or its negation hold.

But apart from differences in detail, the interpretations of the June letter tend to fall into one of two camps: those who see the demise of the theory of knowledge as turning on issues of logical type – Sommerville and Griffin belong here – and those who view the problem as having to do with the unity of the proposition and not directly with the theory of types at all, for example P. M. Hanks. On Sommerville's reading, the collapse of the *Theory of Knowledge* concerns the relationship between the theory of judgement and the logic of *Principia*. On Hank's reading, what caused Russell's project to grind to a halt was connected to type theory only indirectly, and concerns the multiple relation theory itself, not its connection with other doctrines of theories.

Briefly, Sommerville argues that Wittgenstein's January and June letters express the same objection about types in two different ways.[48] In the January letter the condition for a judgement to include type-differences occurs as Wittgenstein's demand that analysis of 'Socrates is mortal' preclude nonsense, while in June the condition for a judgement to include type-differences is expressed as the requirement that 'aRb v ~aRb' follow on its own, without another premise, from 'A judges that aRb'. In June, according to Sommerville, Wittgenstein insists that nothing in Russell's analysis of 'A judges aRb' shows that R relates the right types – in this case, individuals. But he cannot add a premise to the effect that a and b are individuals since then the elementary status of the judgement will depend upon judging, introducing a regress.[49] Entities are the right type when judgements containing them are significant. If the kind of judgement made in asserting xRy of a, b, and so on determines the type of significant arguments to 'xRy' then it is circular for the type of arguments related by R in judging that aRb to determine the kind of judgement made (elementary, etc.).[50] But Russell wants his theory of judgement to justify the hierarchy of judged propositions,[51] and if it doesn't preclude type mistakes, it leaves the ramified theory of types 'without a foundation in Russell's positive theories of propositional meaning'.[52]

Against Sommerville and Griffin, P. W. Hanks writes that 'the real problem' is 'the problem of the unity of the proposition'.[53] Briefly, Hanks argues that there is nothing problematic in facts about what can be judged determining type distinctions since what is meant by this is epistemological – that judgements expose to view what types are able to be combined – and not metaphysical: judging doesn't make objects divide into this or that type. What is problematic is not the relation of the theory of judgement to the theory of types, he argues, but the theory of judgement itself. Consider 'A judges that aRb'. On Russell's theory what A judges is not a proposition but a collection of a, b, and R, but 'judgement is not something that can occur between a subject and two objects and a relation'.[54] On his view, 'when Wittgenstein says that any correct theory of judgement must show that it is impossible to judge nonsense, by "nonsense" he does not mean something that violates type restrictions. Rather, he means something that is not capable of being true or false.'[55] On his view, Wittgenstein points out in June that Russell's theory fails to satisfy the condition that what is judged is a proposition, that is, something that is true or false.

In reconstructing the June letter I suggest that Wittgenstein is pointing out that there can be nothing conditional, if you will, about the unity of proposition, and about what follows from it. It cannot be the case that 'aRb v ~aRb' follows from a belief that aRb, and that the belief or proposition makes sense, on the premise that some further fact, like the neutral fact, exists. But as I have already said, I do not think the June letter is as important to the demise of the *Theory of Knowledge* as is sometimes implied. I believe that rather than ask 'what is Wittgenstein's objection in the June letter?' we should ask 'why does Russell stop work on the *Theory of Knowledge?*' and 'why does he think that Wittgenstein has discovered a new form of fact, a belief fact?' In addressing these last two questions I argued that Russell is unwilling to accept the principle of atomism so long as that requires the elimination of belief facts. He cannot without better reason eliminate a central component of his dualism, for one thing. He has to interpret Wittgenstein's objections as introducing a new form rather than as eliminating the belief fact, even if it means pushing logic and epistemology even closer together. His unwillingness to deny that beliefs are relevant to logic, coupled with having no good idea of how to explain their form or their connection to molecular forms, has the result that, at the point of transition to molecular propositional thought, he stops. Wittgenstein's letter and the subsequent meeting of the two men, I suggest, simply reinforce what Russell has already concluded: that Wittgenstein has shown him the existence of a hitherto unknown form – one with two relations – and that he, Russell, has no idea how to explain how facts of that form are true, or how they are connected to other, more complicated forms.

Conclusion

In the preceding pages I have employed Russell's working notes to clarify the difficulties facing his theory of propositions and judgement. On my reconstruction, Russell struggles to define a proposition because of his realist and atomist theory of meaning, that is, from his conception of judgement as a kind of relational fact. For by focusing on judgements as complexes of meanings he conflates the way a relation occurs in a fact with the way it occurs in a symbol structure. Several problems result, and we have seen some of them in this chapter. One is the difficulty of establishing a coherent account of correspondence; another is the need to treat the relation as holding between items (in order for the judgement to say anything) and the impossibility of its holding (if there are any false beliefs). These problems are related and bear on the June letter.

In catching hold of Wittgenstein's objections as though they were pointing in the direction of new forms, Russell demonstrates something of the scientific spirit, or the spirit of the philosopher who views his task as like a science; progressive, objective and so forth. There is a particular irony in Russell's communications with Ottoline in June, as the book is becoming more and more of a burden. To Ottoline he writes, very much as though trying to look on the bright side, that 'in spite of Wittgenstein, and even if every particular statement in it is false, I am *sure* the book I am writing is a good book, because it gives an example of scientific method where previous writing has been unscientific'.[56] Russell's conviction that 'making certain parts of philosophy scientific' is of value, and that this 'will certainly be the main thing I shall have achieved' is extraordinarily at odds with Wittgenstein's own philosophical sensibilities. This is made very clear to Russell shortly, as the following letter from Wittgenstein shows. In it he writes in order to analyse a quarrel between them and to sever ties with Russell. The quarrel is over the nature of philosophy, specifically, the value of scientific philosophy:

> Our latest quarrell, too, was certainly not simply a result of your sensitiveness or my inconsiderateness. It came from deeper – from the fact that my letter must have shown you how totally different our ideas are, E.G. of the value of a scientific work. It was, of course, stupid of me to have written to you at such length about this matter: I ought to have told myself that such fundamental differences cannot be resolved by a letter. And this is just ONE instance out of *many*. Now, as I'm writing this in complete calm, I can see perfectly well that your value-judgements are just as good and just as deep-seated in you as in me, and that I have no right to catechize you. But I see equally clearly, now, that for that very reason there cannot be any real friendship between us.[57]

It isn't until 1919, when Russell meets with Wittgenstein after the long break in their communication caused by World War I, that he begins to appreciate how differently they view philosophy, and how they have grown in quite opposite directions. By 1919 Wittgenstein's comments in 1912–14 have matured into the views, expressed in the self-deconstructing *Tractatus Logico-Philosophicus* of 1922, that philosophical problems are nonsensical pseudo-science. Ironically, Russell's attempt to absorb Wittgenstein's remarks leads him to promulgate new and increasingly scientifically oriented philosophical doctrines.

Appendix

The following documents are reproduced here by kind permission of the Bertrand Russell Archives at McMaster University, in Hamilton, Ontario, Canada.

1. An outline of the *Theory of Knowledge* manuscript; printed in Bertrand Russell, *Collected Papers of Bertrand Russell*. Vol. VIII: *Theory of Knowledge: The 1913 Manuscript*, ed. Elizabeth Ramsden Eames, in collaboration with Kenneth Blackwell (London: George Allen & Unwin, 1984), 188–9.

2. 'Props': three pages of notes on propositions; printed in ibid., 194–9.

" $x R_y$ " has diff[t] uses:

(1) as the name of the $+^{ve}$ fact $x R_y$

(2) as the name of the neutral prop. or of the neutral fact.

(3) as the expression of a j.

These must be distinguished.

(1) Call the $+^{ve}$ fact $+(x R_y)$, & the $-^{ve}$ fact $-(x R_y)$.

(2) Call the neutral fact $\pm(x R_y)$, & the prop $x R_y$.

(3) Call the j. $J\{+(x R_y)\}$ or $J\{-(x R_y)\}$ or $J\{\pm(x R_y)\}$.

No, this won't do: it must be $+J(x R_y)$, $-J(x R_y)$, $\pm J(x R_y)$.

Otherwise we sh[d] have to know before judging.

Judgment involves the neutral fact, not the $+^{ve}$ or $-^{ve}$ fact.

The neutral fact has a rel[n] to a $+^{ve}$ fact, or to a $-^{ve}$ fact.

J. asserts one of these. It will still be a multiple rel[n], but its terms will not be the same as in my old theory. The neutral fact replaces the form.

Call neutral fact "positively directed" when it corresponds to a $+^{ve}$ fact; "negatively directed" when it corresponds to a $-^{ve}$ fact.

$+^{ve}$ & $-^{ve}$ among facts may be 2 predicates, or a sym[metric] transitive rel[n]: "sameness of sense".

3

Above suits Excluded Middle, but not Contradiction.

$$\pm) \ . = \ \sim (\sim p \lor \sim q) \qquad \sim (\sim p) = p$$

$$\sim (p.q) \ . = \ . \ \sim p \lor \sim q$$

$$\sim (p.\sim p) \ = \ . \ \sim p \lor p .$$

Our allowing $\sim(\sim p) = p$, contrad^n & excluded middle are identical.

Negation. the negation of the $+^{ve}$ or $\sim$ fact is the $\sim$ or $+^{ve}$ fact.

That is the negation of the neutral prop^n or of the neutral fact. Call $+f(xR_3)$ the f of $+xR_3$, etc. Then the negation of a f. is the f of the $\sim$.

The correspondence in $f.$ is between $+f(xR_3) \& +(xR_3))$?

$$\& \ -f(xR_3) \& \sim (xR_3))$$
$$\& \ +f(xR_3) \& + (xR_3))$$

This correspondence, however, entails the old difficulties: it seems not intimate enough. And it suggests dangers of an endless regress. It can't be quite right.

There will only be a neutral fact when the obj^{ts} are of the right types. This introduces great difficulties.

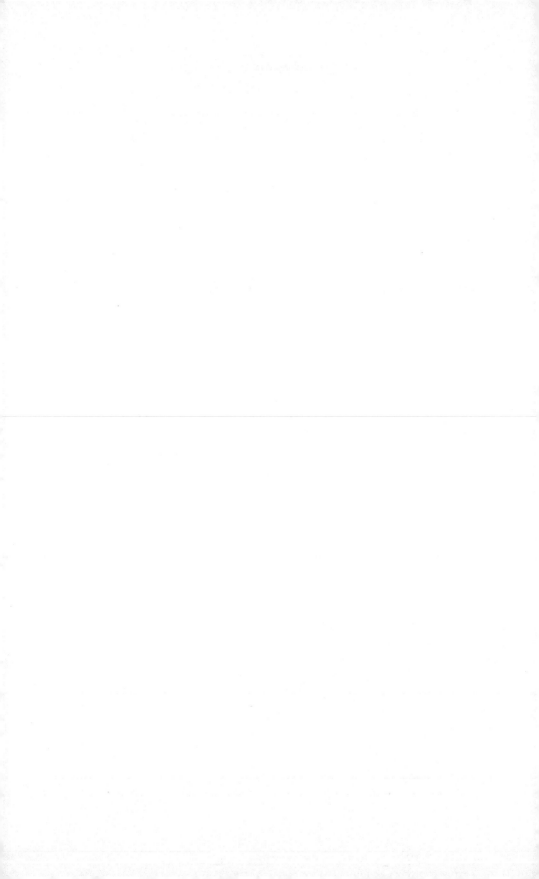

Notes

Introduction

1 Russell to Morrell, Sat. 1916, in Bertrand Russell, *Autobiography of Bertrand Russell: 1914–1944* (London: George Allen & Unwin, 1968), 67–69.

2 Bertrand Russell and Alfred North Whitehead, *Principia Mathematica: to *56* (Cambridge: Cambridge University Press, 1976).

3 A detailed picture of this part of Russell's life has been set forth in Bertrand Russell, *Collected Papers of Bertrand Russell*. Vol. VII: *Theory of Knowledge: The 1913 Manuscript*, ed. Elizabeth Ramsden Eames, with Kenneth Blackwell (London: George Allen & Unwin, 1984), vii–xli; in Bertrand Russell, *Autobiography of Bertrand Russell: 1872–1914* (London: George Allen & Unwin, 1967); in Russell, *Autobiography: 1914–1944* (London: George Allen & Unwin, 1968), 57; in Ray Monk, *Bertrand Russell: The Spirit of Solitude: 1872–1921* (New York: The Free Press, 1996); and in Nicholas Griffin, *Selected Letters of Bertrand Russell* (London: The Penguin Press, 1992).

4 Russell to Morrell, 18 March 1912, in Griffin, *Selected Letters*, 417–19: 'Wittgenstein came and stayed until 12. We had a close passionate discussion of the most difficult point in mathematical philosophy. I think he has *genius* . . . He is the ideal pupil – he gives passionate admiration with vehement and very intelligent dissent . . . He is not a flatterer, but a man of transparent and absolute sincerity . . .'

5 Russell to Morrell, pmk. 23 February 1913, in Griffin, *Selected Letters*, 446–49: '. . . Wittgenstein has persuaded me that the early parts of *Principia Mathematica* are very inexact, but fortunately it is his business to put them right, not mine'.

6 Wittgenstein is commonly read as having rejected Russell's intensionalist logic – a logic in which there are properties, or meanings, over and above classes – in favour of a logic that is extensionalist (there are only classes or sets), nominalist (propositional functions occur extensionally in propositions), and truth-functional (there are no functions of propositions except truth-functions.) In 1925 Russell surrenders his

intensionalist stance, adopts such an extensionalist view, crediting it to Wittgenstein. Russell rejects a theory of types as based on meanings and begins to view it as a doctrine based on extensionalist criteria. As a result, he acknowledges that sentences such as 'A believes that *p*' cannot be taken as functions of *p*. Cf. Russell and Whitehead, *Principia Mathematica: to *56*, xiv.

7 Russell to Morrell, #775, 14 May 1913, cited in Russell, *Papers*, VII, xxvii: '. . . [Wittgenstein is] shocked to hear I am writing on theory of knowledge – he thinks it will be like the shilling book [*Problems of Philosophy*], which he hates . . .'

8 Wittgenstein to Russell; R.12, June 1913, Ludwig Wittgenstein, *Cambridge Letters: Correspondence with Russell, Keynes, Moore, Ramsey and Sraffa*, ed. Brian McGuiness and G. H. von Wright (Oxford: Basil Blackwell, 1995), 29.

9 Russell to Morrell, 19 June 1913, in Griffin, *Selected Letters*, 461–62: 'All that has gone wrong with me lately comes from Wittgenstein's attack on my work – I have only just realized this. It was very difficult to be honest about it, as it makes a large part of the book I meant to write impossible for years to come probably. I tried to believe it wasn't so bad as that . . . And the failure of honesty over my work . . . spread poison . . .'

10 Wittgenstein to Russell; R.13, Wittgenstein, *Cambridge Letters*, 29: '. . . I am very sorry to hear that my objection to your theory of judgement paralyses you. I think it can only be removed by a correct theory of propositions.'

11 For a detailed and persuasive study of the workings of Wittgenstein's thought prior to the coming together of his ideas initiated by his objections to Russell's 1913 manuscript, see Stephen Sommerville, 'Types, Categories and Significance' (PhD thesis, McMaster University, 1979).

12 For further details concerning Russell's plans for the manuscript, see Russell, *Papers*, VII, xxii–xxiv and appendices.

13 For additional information on revisions and publication of parts of the text see Russell, *Papers*, VII, vii–xlvii and the appendices.

14 Communication between Wittgenstein and Russell breaks off after 22 October 1915 not to resume until 2 September 1919. Cf. Wittgenstein, *Cambridge Letters*, 103–7.

15 Russell, *Papers*, VII, 46.

16 Russell has in mind the occurrence of a belief or perception, say, the fact, A's belief that Othello loves Desdemona. Such facts, he thinks, have an essential reference to the subject who believes (or perceives).

17 I agree with Eames, who sees Russell as showing Wittgenstein's influence by 'the dropping out the subject's relation of belief of judgement to what is believed in favor of treating the proposition as

unaffected'. Elizabeth Ramsden Eames, *Bertrand Russell's Dialogue with His Contemporaries* (Carbondale and Edwardsville: Southern Illinois University Press, 1989), 161.

18 Ludwig Wittgenstein, 'Notes on Logic', in *Notebooks 1914–1916*, 2nd edn, ed. G. H. von Wright and G. E. M. Anscombe, with an English translation by G. E. M. Anscombe (Oxford: Basil Blackwell, 1979), 94.

19 Ibid., 96.

20 Ludwig Wittgenstein, 'Logische-Philosophische Abhandlung' in *Annalen der Naturphilosophie*, no. 14, Leibzig, 1921; first published in English under the title *Tractatus Logico-Philosophicus*, trans. C. K. Ogden and F. P. Ramsey, with an introduction by Bertrand Russell (London: Routledge & Kegan Paul, 1922; reprinted with corrections 1933), 149.

Chapter 1

1 Bertrand Russell, 'Meinong's Theory of Complexes and Assumptions', in *Essays in Analysis*, ed. D. Lackey (New York: George Allen & Unwin, 1973), 21–22; reprinted in *Collected Papers of Bertrand Russell.* Vol. IV: *Foundations of Logic: 1903–05*, ed. Alasdair Urquehart, with the assistance of Albert C. Lewis (London: Routledge, 1994), 432.

2 Bertrand Russell, 'Knowledge by Acquaintance and Knowledge by Description', in *Mysticism and Logic and Other Essays* (London: Longmans, Green and Co., 1918), 220; reprinted in Bertrand Russell, *Collected Papers of Bertrand Russell*, Vol. VI: *Logical and Philosophical Papers: 1909–13*, ed. John G. Slater, with the assistance of Bernd Frohmann (London: Routledge, 1992).

3 See, for example, Bertrand Russell, 'On Fundamentals', in *Collected Papers of Bertrand Russell*, Vol. IV: *Foundations of Logic: 1903–05*, ed. Alasdair Urquehart, with the assistance of Albert C. Lewis (London: Routledge, 1994), 359–413.

4 Bertrand Russell, 'On Denoting', in *Logic and Knowledge: Essays, 1901–1950*, ed. R. Marsh (London: George Allen & Unwin, 1956), 49; reprinted in Russell, *Papers*, IV, 415–27.

5 Bertrand Russell and A. N. Whitehead, *Principia Mathematica: to *56* (Cambridge: Cambridge University Press, 1976), 66.

6 Russell remarks in *Principia*, 48: 'A proposition is not a single entity, but a relation of several; hence a statement in which a proposition appears as subject will only be significant if it can be reduced to a statement about the terms which appear in the proposition. A proposition, like phrases "the so-and-so", where grammatically it appears as subject, must be broken up into its constituents if we are to find the true subject or subjects.'

7 Russell, 'Meinong's Theory of Complexes and Assumptions', in *Papers*, IV, 432.

8 Russell, 'Points about Denoting', in *Papers*, IV, 307.

9 Russell and Whitehead, *Principia*, 41.

10 Russell, 'Meinong's Theory of Complexes and Assumptions', in *Papers*, IV, 443.

11 Ibid., 447.

12 Bertrand Russell, *Principles of Mathematics* (Cambridge: Cambridge University Press, 1903), 12–13.

13 For further instructive discussion of the theory of types see Alonzo Church, 'Comparison of Russell's Resolution of the Semantical Antinomies with that of Tarski', *Journal of Symbolic Logic* 41 (1976), 747–60; Kurt Gödel, 'Russell's Mathematical Logic', in *The Philosophy of Bertrand Russell*, The Library of Living Philosophers, 5, ed. Paul Schilpp (La Salle, IL: Open Court Press, 1944), 123–53; Warren Goldfarb, 'Russell's Reasons for Ramification', in *Minnesota Studies in the Philosophy of Science*, Vol. XII, *Rereading Russell: Essays on Bertrand Russell's Metaphysics and Epistemology*, ed. C. Wade Savage and C. Anthony Anderson (Minneapolis: University of Minnesota Press, 1989), 24–40; Peter Hylton, 'Russell's Substitutional Theory', *Synthese* 45 (1980), 1–31; Gregory Landini, *Russell's Hidden Substitutional Theory* (Oxford: Oxford University Press, 1998); W. V. O. Quine, 'Russell's Ontological Development', *Journal of Philosophy* 63 (21) (1966), 657–67; and Frank P. Ramsey, *Philosophical Papers*, ed. D. H. Mellor (Cambridge: Cambridge University Press, 1990).

14 Russell's theory of types in the *Principles*, his use of the techniques in 'On Denoting' to eliminate classes, functions and relations as entities, his substitutional theory, the question of whether he drops this approach or integrates it in the version of the type theory employed in *Principles* are topics of considerable interest among many that I cannot pursue here.

15 Other relevant notes include Bertrand Russell, 'Logic in which Propositions are Not Entities' (May 1906) and Bertrand Russell, 'The Paradox of Logic' (June 1906).

16 Bertrand Russell, 'The Paradox of the Liar', #11, unpublished manuscript, 2.

17 Ibid., 3.

18 Russell, 'Meinong's Theory of Complexes and Assumptions', in *Papers*, IV, 447.

19 Russell, 'The Paradox of the Liar', 3.

20 Bertrand Russell, 'Types', #18a, unpublished manuscript, 141.

21 Ibid., 142.

22 Bertrand Russell, 'On the Nature of Truth', *Proceedings of the Aristotelian*

Society (1906), 28–49. Russell expresses doubts about the theory, and when he reprints the paper in 1910 as 'The Monistic Theory of Truth' he leaves out the section containing the doctrine, while adding a different version in a new paper titled 'On the Nature of Truth and Falsehood' (Russell, *Philosophical Essays* (London: George Allen & Unwin, 1910; revised 1966), 147–59). The 1910 paper marks Russell's first public adoption of the multiple relation theory. In 'Knowledge by Acquaintance and Knowledge by Description', referring to his 1910 theory of judgement in *Philosophical Essays*, Russell mistakenly cites 'The Nature of Truth'.

23 Ibid., 46.
24 Russell, 'On the Nature of Truth', *Proc. Arist. Society*, 46. Russell's papers on truth are easily confused. On 11 June 1904 Russell read 'Nature of Truth' to the Sunday Essay Society; this is now published in Russell, *Papers*, IV, 491. On 10 June 1905 he read a still unpublished paper 'Nature of Truth' to the Jowett Society. A different paper called 'The Nature of Truth' appears in a 1906 issue of *Mind*. In May of 1906 Russell completed 'On the Nature of Truth', a three-part paper. This is a paper he read twice, once on 2 November 1906 to the Cambridge Moral Sciences Club and once on 4 December 1906 to the Aristotelian Society. This is the paper published in the 1906–07 *Proceedings of the Aristotelian Society*.
25 Russell, 'The Paradox of the Liar', 63.
26 Ibid., 4.
27 Ibid.
28 Russell, 'Types', 141.
29 Ibid.
30 Frank Ramsey, *Philosophical Papers*, ed. D. H. Mellor (Cambridge: Cambridge University Press, 1990), 34.
31 Ibid., 49.
32 Ibid., 48.
33 Russell, 'Meinong's Theory of Complexes and Assumptions', in *Papers*, IV, 473.
34 Russell, 'On the Nature of Truth and Falsehood', in *Philosophical Essays*, 149.
35 Bertrand Russell, 'Meinong's Theory of Complexes and Assumptions', *Papers*, IV, 473.
36 Russell, 'The Nature of Truth', *Papers*, IV, 493.
37 Griffin argues Russell's 1906 theory of belief introduces a multiple relation of judging. Nicholas Griffin, 'Russell on the Nature of Logic (1903–1913)', *Synthese* 45 (1980), 117–88.

38 Russell, 'On the Nature of Truth', *Proc. Arist. Society*, 46–47.

39 Bertrand Russell, 'Transatlantic Truth', reprinted as 'William James's Conception of Truth', in *Philosophical Essays*, 132, 137–38.

40 Russell, 'William James's Conception of Truth', in *Philosophical Essays*, 144.

41 Ibid., 152.

42 Russell, 'On the Nature of Truth', 43.

43 Russell, *Papers*, VII, 80.

44 Ibid., 140.

45 Russell, 'Knowledge by Acquaintance and Knowledge by Description', in *Mysticism and Logic*, 230. I cannot discuss here the history behind Russell's acceptance of sense data.

46 For a discussion of inner sense see Bertrand Russell, *Problems of Philosophy* (Oxford: Oxford University Press, 1912), 19 and 49.

47 Russell, *Problems*, 48–49. Without this knowledge, according to Russell, we could not know the past by inference, because we wouldn't know that there was anything to infer.

48 Cf. ibid., 97.

49 Russell and Whitehead, *Principia*, 43.

50 Ibid.

51 Ibid.

52 Russell, *Problems*, 137.

53 Russell, *Papers*, VII, 168.

54 Russell and Whitehead, *Principia*, 39.

55 The literature on the status of Russellian propositional functions is vast. The reader will find some of it listed in the bibliography.

56 Russell and Whitehead, *Principia*, 39.

57 Ibid., 44.

58 Ibid.

59 Ibid., 45.

60 Ibid., 42.

61 Russell, 'On the Nature of Truth and Falsehood', in *Philosophical Essays*, 158.

62 G. F. Stout, *Studies in Philosophy and Psychology* (London: Macmillan, 1930), 239–57; reprint from *Proc. Arist. Society* (1911), 181ff.

63 Citation taken from Nicholas Griffin, 'Russell's Multiple-Relation Theory of Judgement', *Philosophical Studies* 47 (1985), 220.

64 Russell, *Problems*, 127.

65 Russell, *Principles*, 228.

66 Ibid., 449.

67 Ibid., 228.

68 Ibid., 116.

69 David Pears, *Bertrand Russell and the British Tradition in Philosophy* (London: Fontana Press, 1967).

70 Russell, *Papers* 6, 55–56. It is of course possible that we are seeing Wittgenstein's influence on Russell already in this short manuscript.

71 Ibid., 55.

72 Ibid., 56.

73 Ibid.

74 Ibid.

75 Excerpted in Russell, *Papers*, VI, 53.

76 Russell, *Papers*, VII, 46.

77 Ludwig Wittgenstein, *Ludwig Wittgenstein: Cambridge Letters, Correspondence with Russell, Keynes, Moore, Ramsey and Sraffa*, ed. Brian McGuinness and G. H. von Wright (Oxford: Basil Blackwell, 1995), 24.

78 Wittgenstein to Russell, R. 9, Allegasse, Vienna, January 1913, in ibid., 23.

79 Ibid. Note that '[A]' and '[B]' do not appear in the original text.

80 Ibid.

81 Stephen Sommerville writes (in 'Types, Categories and Significance', unpublished PhD thesis, McMaster University, 1979, 694): 'The difference between Russell's "$\phi(x)$" and Wittgenstein's "$(\exists x,y)\ \varepsilon_1(x,y)$" would be accountable to Wittgenstein's having treated a copula of this type as having a form which relates two *named* items (Socrates, Mortality) and to his insistence that only apparent (bound) variables occur in the forms of logical propositions.' He has in mind Wittgenstein's contention that logical propositions contain only apparent variables.

82 Griffin, 'Russell's Multiple Relation Theory of Judgement', 229.

83 Nicholas Griffin, 'Russell on the Nature of Logic (1903–1913)', 171.

84 Ibid.

Chapter 2

1 Bertrand Russell, *Collected Papers of Bertrand Russell.* Vol. VII: *Theory of Knowledge: The 1913 Manuscript*, ed. Elizabeth Ramsden Eames in collaboration with Kenneth Blackwell (London: George Allen & Unwin, 1984), xxvii.

2 Russell to Morrell, 20 May 1913, excerpted and cited in ibid., xxvii.

3 Letter #785; cited in Elizabeth Ramsden Eames, *Bertrand Russell's Dialogue with His Contemporaries* (Carbondale and Edwardsville, IL: Southern Illinois University Press, 1989), 147.

4 Eames, *Bertrand Russell's Dialogue*, 146.

5 Labelled A. 4 in the appendix to Russell, *Papers*, VII, 186–87.

6 Nicholas Griffin, 'Russell's Multiple Relation Theory of Judgement', *Philosophical Studies* 47 (1985), 227–28.

7 Ibid.

8 Ludwig Wittgenstein, *Notebooks 1914–1916*, ed. G.H. von Wright and G. E. M. Anscombe, with an English translation by G. E. M. Anscombe (Oxford: Basil Blackwell, 1979), 98.

9 Bertrand Russell, 'Knowledge by Acquaintance and Knowledge by Description', in *Mysticism and Logic* (London: Longmans, Green and Co., 1918), 159*n*.

10 Russell to Morrell, #775, 14 May 1913, cited in Russell, *Papers*, VII, xxvii.

11 Bertrand Russell, *Problems of Philosophy* (Oxford: Oxford University Press, 1912), 127.

12 Russell to Morrell, 20 May 1913, excerpted and cited in Russell, *Papers*, VII, xxvii: '. . . [Wittgenstein came with] a refutation of the theory of judgement which I used to hold. He was right, but I think the correction required is not very serious. I shall have to make up my mind within a week, as I shall soon reach [the chapter on] judgement . . .'

13 Bertrand Russell, *Principles of Mathematics* (Cambridge: Cambridge University Press, 1903), 225.

14 Ricketts discusses this issue, pointing out that we can detect Wittgenstein's hand in Russell's decision in *Theory of Knowledge* to reject his 1903 view that 'a before b' and 'b after a' are objectively different. See Thomas Ricketts, 'Pictures, Logic, and the Limits of Sense in Wittgenstein's *Tractatus*', in *Cambridge Companion to Wittgenstein*, ed. H. Sluga and D. Stern (Cambridge: Cambridge University Press, 1996), 67.

15 Russell, *Papers*, VII, 89.

16 Bertrand Russell, 'What is Logic?' in *Collected Papers of Bertrand Russell*, Vol. VI: *Logical and Philosophical Papers*, ed. John G. Slater, with the assistance of Bernd Frohmann (London: Routledge, 1992), 56.

17 The issue is analogous to that of explaining how a proposition and its complement – the two sides of what is really one proposition – can have the same meaning but different senses. Both the problem of sense as it applies to asymmetrical relations and the problem as it pertains to the polarity of a proposition press towards an account of what underlies the distinctions we use language to make and therefore cannot be explained in that language.

18 Griffin ('Russell's Multiple Relation Theory of Judgement', 231) cites p. 146 of the *Theory of Knowledge* as evidence that Russell reverses his point that the terms are functions of the relating relation, saying that the terms are not functions of the relating relation.

19 Russell, *Papers*, VII, 111.

20 Ibid., 79.

21 Wittgenstein, 'Notes on Logic', in *Notebooks*, 97.

22 Wittgenstein, *Notebooks*, 48.

23 Russell denies that logical objects are constituents in 'What is Logic?', *Papers*, VI, 55.

24 Russell, *Papers*, VII, 98.

25 Ibid.

26 The term appears on the outline found with Russell's manuscript. Cf. appendix A.5 in Russell, *Papers*, VII.

27 Russell, *Papers*, VII, 97.

28 Ibid., 116.

29 Ibid.

30 Ibid.

31 Ibid.,

32 Ibid., 112.

33 Ibid., 112.

34 Ibid., 135.

35 Ibid.

36 Eames, *Bertrand Russell's Dialogue*, 149.

37 Stephen Sommerville, 'Types, Categories and Significance' (unpublished PhD thesis, McMaster University, 1979), 690–94.

38 Labelled A.4 in the appendix to Russell, *Papers*, VII, 186–87.

39 Published as appendix A.4 in ibid., 186; see the appendix to the present volume for reproductions of the notes in which these diagrams appear.

40 Ibid., 187.

41 Russell to Ottoline Morrell, #785; cited in Eames, *Bertrand Russell's Dialogue*, 147.

42 For the outline and drafts see Bertrand Russell, *Papers*, VII, 188–89 and 200. For the editors' notes concerning the relations among these notes and diagrams see ibid., 181, 187 and 189.

43 Eames, *Bertrand Russell's Dialogue*, 147. Her reconstruction of the outline and diagram A.5 seems to me to be correct. Note that her supporting footnote (on 253) cites as the diagram on the verso of the outline A.5 the diagram A.4, rather than the one that is found there: diagram B.2.

44 Russell, *Papers*, VII, 114.

45 Ibid., 109.

46 Ibid., 107.

47 Ibid.

48 Ibid., 25.

49 Ibid.

50 Russell argues that mental entities must exist because it is 'impossible' to think of an abstract fact 'unless it contains some constituent over and above the timeless thing thought of or believed' (ibid., 32).

51 Ibid., 108.

52 Ibid.

53 Ibid.

54 Ibid., 113.

55 Ibid., 118.

56 Ibid., 200.

57 Ibid.

58 Bertrand Russell, *Collected Papers of Bertrand Russell*, Vol. VIII: *The Philosophy of Logical Atomism and Other Essays, 1914–1919*, ed. John G. Slater (London: George Allen & Unwin, 1986), 198–99.

59 Russell, *Papers*, VII, 40.

60 Ibid., 37.

61 Ibid.

62 Ibid., 115–17.

63 Ibid., 98.

64 Wittgenstein, *Notebooks*, 17.

Chapter 3

1 Nicholas Griffin, *Selected Letters of Bertrand Russell* (London: Penguin Press, 1992), 459.

2 Bertrand Russell, *Collected Papers of Bertrand Russell*, Vol. VII: *Theory of Knowledge: The 1913 Manuscript*, ed. Elizabeth Ramsden Eames, with Kenneth Blackwell (London: George Allen & Unwin, 1984), 119.

3 Ibid.

4 Ibid., 124.

5 Ludwig Wittgenstein, *Tractatus Logico Philosophicus*, trans. C. K. Ogden and F. P. Ramsey, introduction by Bertrand Russell (London: Routledge & Kegan Paul, 1922), 63.

6 Russell, *Papers*, VII, 127.

7 Ibid., 131.

8 Russell, *Papers*, VIII, 200.

9 David Pears, *Bertrand Russell and the British Tradition in Philosophy* (London: Fontana Press, 1967), 188ff.

10 Russell, *Papers*, VII, 128.

11 Ibid., 122.

12 Ibid., 128.

13 Ibid.

14 Ibid.

15 Ludwig Wittgenstein, *Cambridge Letters: Correspondence with Russell, Keynes, Moore, Ramsey and Sraffa*, ed. B. McGuiness and G. H. von Wright (Oxford: Basil Blackwell, 1995), 14.

16 Russell, *Papers*, VII, 132.

17 Ibid., 99.

18 Ibid., 130.

19 Ludwig Wittgenstein, 'Notes on Logic', in *Notebooks 1914–1916*, ed. G. H. von Wright and G. E. M. Anscombe, trans. G. E. M. Anscombe (Oxford: Basil Blackwell, 1979), 100–1.

20 Russell, *Papers*, VII, 130.

21 Ibid. Cf. Wittgenstein, 'Notes on Logic', in *Notebooks*, 97.

22 Ibid., 130.

23 Ibid., 133.

24 Ibid.

25 Ibid., 134.

26 Ibid.

27 Ibid., 135.

28 See the appendix to this text for a reproduction of the outline in question.

29 Ibid., 136. I ignore Russell's polemic against Idealism and neutral monism as irrelevant to my present aim of examining Wittgenstein's impact on the text.

30 Ibid.

31 Bertrand Russell, *The Collected Papers of Bertrand Russell*, Vol. VIII: *The Philosophy of Logical Atomism and Other Essays, 1914–1919*, ed. John G. Slater (London: George Allen & Unwin, 1986), 187.

32 In 1918 Russell says that truth and falsity are properties of sentences but that for formal purposes it is convenient to treat truth as a property of propositions. Russell, *Papers*, VIII, 165. Also printed in Bertrand Russell, *The Philosophy of Logical Atomism*, edited and with an introduction by David Pears (La Salle, IL: Open Court, 1985), 43.

33 Russell, *Papers*, VII, 144.

34 Ibid., 134–35.

35 Ibid., 151.

36 Ibid., 154.

37 Ibid., 184.

38 Ibid., 153.

39 Ibid., 154.

40 Ludwig Wittgenstein, *Tractatus Logico-Philosophicus*, trans. C. K. Ogden and F. P. Ramsey, introduction by Bertrand Russell (London: Routledge & Kegan Paul, 1922), 63.

41   Russell, *Papers*, VII, 154.
42   Ibid., 153.
43   Ibid., 155.
44   Ibid., 156.
45   Ibid., 157.
46   Ibid.
47   Ibid., 161.
48   Ibid., 161.
49   Ibid.,
50   Ibid.
51   Ibid., 165.
52   Ibid., 162.
53   Ibid., 159.
54   Ibid.
55   Ibid.
56   Ibid.
57   Russell to Morrell, 18 March 1912, in Griffin, *Selected Letters*, 417–18.
58   Ibid., 10.
59   Ibid., 11.
60   Ibid., 34.
61   Russell, *Papers*, VII, 167.

Chapter 4

1   Bertrand Russell, *Collected Papers of Bertrand Russell*, Vol. VII: *Theory of Knowledge: The 1913 Manuscript*, ed. Elizabeth Eames in collaboration with Kenneth Blackwell (London: George Allen & Unwin, 1984), 46.
 2   Russell to Morrell, 28 May 1913, excerpted and cited in Ray Monk, *Bertrand Russell: The Spirit of Solitude, 1872–1921* (New York: The Free Press, 1996), 298.
 3   Russell to Morrell, 1 June 1913, excerpted and cited in ibid.
 4   In 1917 Russell still seems to think the theory of judgement requires only some correcting, not a thorough overhaul. Consider his note to 'Knowledge by Acquaintance and Knowledge by Description' in *Mysticism and Logic* (London: Longmans, Green and Co., 1918), 159*n*: 'I have been persuaded by Mr. Wittgenstein that this theory is somewhat unduly simple, but the modification which I believe it to require does not affect the above argument.'
 5   'Props' occurs as appendix to the present volume and a typescript appears in Russell, *Papers*, VII, 194–99. See different interpretations of 'Props' in Stephen Sommerville, 'Types, Categories and Significance' (unpublished PhD thesis, McMaster University, 1979) and Herbert

Hochberg, 'Propositions, Truth and Belief: the Wittgenstein–Russell Dispute', *Theoria* 66 (2000), 36.

6 Russell, *Papers*, VII, 195.

7 Ibid.

8 Kenneth Blackwell, 'Wittgenstein's Impact on Russell's Theory of Belief' (MA thesis, McMaster University, 1974), 85.

9 While these notes evidently mark a move away from his analysis of understanding, it is difficult to say whether they simply replace understanding with something like the notion of complex perception, since that notion is difficult to categorize even in *Theory of Knowledge*, where it is said to have something in common with dual relations and multiple ones.

10 See the appendix to the present volume and Russell, *Papers*, VII, 195.

11 Russell, *Papers*, VII, 195.

12 Sommerville ('Types, Categories and Significance', 716) sees 'it looks as if there actually were always a relation' as an admission that Russell is committing himself problematically to objective propositions; that is, he thinks that Russell sees that 'if the proposition had to be reintroduced as a genuine constituent of a judgment, belief, or assertion, all of his previous problems . . . over the subsistence of false propositions . . . might recur'.

13 Russell, *Papers*, VII, 197.

14 Ibid., 116.

15 Ibid., 197.

16 Cf. Bertrand Russell, *Collected Papers of Bertrand Russell*, Vol. VIII: *The Philosophy of Logical Atomism and Other Essays* (London: George Allen & Unwin, 1986), 266.

17 Ibid.

18 Russell, *Papers*, VII, 197

19 Ibid, 199.

20 Ibid.

21 Ibid.

22 Ibid.

23 Ibid., 153.

24 Sommerville ('Types, Categories and Significance', 719) thinks that Russell worries that making negative and positive facts on a par, *qua* facts, puts him back in the situation he deplored in 1904, when true and false was, like red and white, the end of the matter, and he thinks that Russell intends the neutral fact (the relation of x, y, R) to be a constituent of the fact; but if it is, there threatens to be a new relation of this relation, and so forth, and a problem of regress threatens. The

regress issue arises, Sommerville thinks, because the neutral fact is supposed to be an actual not a merely logical entity and therefore can't, like logical form, be distinguished from genuine constituents related to other constituents.

25 Russell, *Papers*, VII, 199.

26 Russell, *Papers*, VIII, 199.

27 Ibid., 198.

28 Ibid.

29 Printed in the appendix to the present volume and in Russell, *Papers*, VII, 194.

30 Printed in the appendix to the present volume and in ibid., 196.

31 Ludwig Wittgenstein, 'Notes on Logic', in *Notebooks, 1914–1916*, ed. G. H. von Wright and G. E. M. Anscombe; trans. G. E. M. Anscombe (Oxford: Basil Blackwell, 1979), 106.

32 Russell, *Papers*, VIII, 167.

33 Wittgenstein, *Notebooks*, 95.

34 Russell, *Papers*, VII, 46*n*.

35 Ibid.

36 Ibid.

37 Ludwig Wittgenstein, *Tractatus Logico-Philosophicus*, trans. C. K. Ogden and F. P. Ramsey, with an introduction by Bertrand Russell (London: Routledge & Kegan Paul, 1922).

38 Bertrand Russell, *Our Knowledge of the External World as a Field for Scientific Philosophy* (London: George Allen & Unwin, 1914; revised 1926, 1952), 53.

39 Ibid.

40 Brian McGuinness, 'Bertrand Russell and Ludwig Wittgenstein's "Notes on Logic"', *Internationale de Philosophie* 26 (1972), 448.

41 Bertand Russell, 'On Propositions', in *Papers*, VIII, 294–95: 'The theory of belief which I formerly advocated, namely, that it consisted in a multiple relation of the subject to the objects constituting the "objective", i.e., the fact that makes the belief true or false, is rendered impossible by the rejection of the subject. The constituents of the belief cannot, when the subject is rejected, be the same as the constituents of its "objective"'. Cf. Bertrand Russell, *My Philosophical Development* (London: George Allen & Unwin, 1959), 182: '. . . I abandoned this theory, both because I ceased to believe in the 'subject', and because I no longer thought that a relation can occur significantly as a term, except when a paraphrase is possible in which it does not so occur'.

42 Bertrand Russell, *Papers*, VII, 255.

43 Russell, *Papers*, VII, 198–99.

44 Russell to Morrell, Trinity College, 27 May 1913, in Nicholas Griffin, *Selected Letters of Bertrand Russell* (London: Penguin Press, 1992), 459–60.

45 Ludwig Wittgenstein, *Cambridge Letters: Correspondence with Russell, Keynes, Moore, Ramsey and Sraffa*, ed. Brian McGuiness and G. H. von Wright (Oxford: Basil Blackwell, 1995), 29.

46 See, for example, Nicholas Griffin, 'Russell on the Nature of Logic (1903–1913)', *Synthese* 45, (1980) 117–88 and 'Russell's Multiple Relation Theory of Judgement', *Philosophical Studies* 47 (1985), 227–28; Peter Hylton, *Russell, Idealism and the Emergence of Analytic Philosophy* (Oxford: Clarendon Press, 1990), 357–61; and Stephen Sommerville, 'Types, Categories and Significance' (unpublished PhD thesis, McMaster University, 1979) and 'Wittgenstein to Russell (July, 1913): "I Am Very Sorry to Hear . . . My Objection Paralyses You"', in R. Haller and W. Grassl (eds), *Language, Logic, and Philosophy: Proceedings of the Fourth International Wittgenstein Symposium* (Vienna: Holder-Pichler-Tempsky, 1980), 62–75.

47 Wittgenstein, *Cambridge Letters*, 33.

48 Sommerville, 'Types, Categories and Significance', 701–2.

49 Ibid.

50 Ibid., 706.

51 Ibid., 703.

52 Ibid., 703–4.

53 P. W. Hanks, 'Wittgenstein's Objection to Russell's Multiple Relation Theory of Judgment', *Synthese*, forthcoming.

54 Ibid.

55 Ibid.

56 Russell to Morrell, 1 June 1913, cited in Monk, *Bertrand Russell*, 298.

57 Wittgenstein to Russell, R.26, Norway, February 1914, ibid., 74–75.

58 For a description of Russell's meeting with Wittgenstein in the Hague, see Monk, *Bertrand Russell*, 567–68. For Russell's view of their differences, see 'The Impact of Wittgenstein', in Bertrand Russell, *My Philosophical Development* (London: George Allen & Unwin, 1959), 110–27; and Ludwig Wittgenstein, *Tractatus Logico-Philosophicus*, trans. C. K. Ogden and F. P. Ramsey, with an introduction by Bertrand Russell (London: Routledge & Kegan Paul, 1922), 18.

Bibliography

1. Works by Bertrand Russell

Russell, Bertrand. 1900. *A Critical Exposition of the Philosophy of Leibniz.* Cambridge: Cambridge University Press.

_____. 1903. *The Principles of Mathematics.* Cambridge: Cambridge University Press.

_____. 1906. 'Les paradoxes du logique', *Revue de métaphysique et de morale* 14, 627–50. Reprinted in English as 'On "insolubilia" and their solution by symbolic logic', in Russell 1973, 165–89.

_____. 1910. *Philosophical Essays.* London: Longmans, Green (revised edition, London: George Allen & Unwin, 1966).

_____. 1911a. 'L'importance philosophique de la logistique', *Revue de métaphysique et de morale* 19, 281–91. English translation Russell 1913; reprinted in Russell 1973, 284–94, and in Russell 1992a, 33–40.

_____. 1911b. 'Le réalisme analytique', *Bulletin de la société française de philosophie* 11, 53–82. Reprinted in Russell 1992a, 133–46.

_____. 1911c. 'Sur les axiomes de l'infini et du transfini', *Société mathématique de France: Comptes rendus des séances*, no. 2, 22–35. Trans. 'On the axioms of the infinite and of the transfinite', in Grattan-Guinness 1977, 161–74.

_____. 1912. *The Problems of Philosophy.* Oxford: Oxford University Press.

_____. 1913. 'The philosophical importance of mathematical logic', trans. P. Jourdain. *Monist* 23, 481–93. Reprinted in Russell 1973, 284–94, and Russell 1992a, 33–40.

_____. 1914. *Our Knowledge of the External World as a Field for Scientific Method in Philosophy.* Chicago: Open Court (revised edition, London: Allen & Unwin, 1926).

_____. 1918. *Mysticism and Logic.* London: Longmans, Green and Co.

_____. 1919a. *Introduction to Mathematical Philosophy.* London: George Allen & Unwin.

_____. 1919b. 'On propositions: what they are and how they mean', *Proceedings of the Aristotelian Society*, Sup. Vol. 2, 1–43. Reprinted in Russell 1956, 283–320.

_____. 1920. 'The meaning of "meaning"', *Mind* 29, 398–401. Reprinted in Russell 1988.

_____. 1921. *Analysis of Mind.* London: George Allen & Unwin.

_____. 1927. *Analysis of Matter.* London: Kegan Paul.

_____. 1940. *Inquiry into Meaning and Truth.* New York: W. W. Norton.

_____. 1948. *Human Knowledge: Its Scope and Limits.* London: George Allen and Unwin.

_____. 1956. *Logic and Knowledge: Essays, 1901–1950.* Ed. R. Marsh. London: George Allen & Unwin.

_____. 1959. *My Philosophical Development.* London: George Allen & Unwin.

_____. 1967. *Autobiography of Bertrand Russell: 1872–1914.* London: George Allen & Unwin.

_____. 1968. *Autobiography of Bertrand Russell: 1914–1944.* London: George Allen & Unwin.

_____. 1973. *Essays in Analysis.* Ed. D. Lackey. London: George Allen & Unwin.

_____. 1984. *Theory of Knowledge: The 1913 Manuscript.* Collected Papers of Bertrand Russell, Vol. VII. Ed. Elizabeth Ramsden Eames in collaboration with Kenneth Blackwell. London: George Allen & Unwin.

_____. 1985. *Philosophy of Logical Atomism.* Ed. and intro. David Pears. La Salle, IL: Open Court.

_____. 1986. *The Philosophy of Logical Atomism and Other Essays, 1914–1919.* Collected Papers of Bertrand Russell, Vol. VIII. Ed. John G. Slater. London: George Allen & Unwin.

_____. 1988. *Essays on Language, Mind, and Matter, 1919–26.* Collected Papers of Bertrand Russell, Vol. IX. Ed. John G. Slater. London: Unwin Hyman.

_____. 1992a. *Logical and Philosophical Papers: 1909–13.* Collected Papers of Bertrand Russell, Vol. VI. Ed. John G. Slater with the assistance of Bernd Frohmann. London: George Allen & Unwin.

_____. 1992b. *The Selected Letters of Bertrand Russell.* Vol. I: *The Private Years (1884–1914).* Ed. Nicholas Griffin. London: Penguin.

_____. 1994. *Foundations of Logic: 1903–05.* Collected Papers of Bertrand Russell, Vol. IV. Ed. Alasdair Urquhart with the assistance of Albert C. Lewis. London and New York: Routledge.

Russell, Bertrand and Alfred North Whitehead. 1976. *Principia Mathematica to *56.* Cambridge: Cambridge University Press.

2. Works by Ludwig Wittgenstein

Engelman, Paul. 1967. *Letters from Ludwig Wittgenstein with a Memoir.* Ed. B. F. McGuinness. Trans. L. Furthmiller. Oxford: Basil Blackwell.

Wittgenstein, Ludwig. 1922. *Tractatus Logico-Philosophicus.* Trans. C. K. Ogden and F. P. Ramsey, intro. Bertrand Russell. London: Routledge & Kegan Paul.

_____. 1961. *Tractatus Logico-Philosophicus.* Trans. David F. Pears and Brian F. McGuinness, intro. Bertrand Russell. London: Routledge & Kegan Paul.

_____. 1971. *Prototractatus: An Early Version of Tractatus Logico-Philosophicus.* Ed. B. F. McGuinness, T. Nyberg and G. H. von Wright, trans. D. F. Pears and B. F. McGuinness. Oxford: Basil Blackwell.

_____. 1973. *Letters to C. K. Ogden with Comments on the English Translation of the Tractatus-Logico-Philosophicus.* Edited with an introduction by G. H. von Wright and with an appendix of letters by Frank Plumpton Ramsey. Oxford: Basil Blackwell.

_____. 1975. *Philosophical Remarks.* Ed. Rush Rhees, trans. Raymond Hargreaves and Roger White. Chicago: University of Chicago Press.

_____. 1979. *Notebooks 1914–1916,* 2nd edn. Ed. G. H. von Wright and G. E. M. Anscombe, trans. G. E. M. Anscombe. Oxford: Basil Blackwell.

_____. 1995. *Ludwig Wittgenstein: Cambridge Letters, Correspondence with Russell, Keynes, Moore, Ramsey and Sraffa.* Ed. Brian McGuinness and G. H. von Wright. Oxford: Basil Blackwell.

3. Works by Others

Ammerman, Robert R. (ed). 1965. *Classics of Analytic Philosophy.* New York: McGraw-Hill.

Anscombe, G. E. M. 1971. *An Introduction to Wittgenstein's Tractatus,* 4th edn. London: Hutchinson.

Armstrong, D. M. 2000. 'Difficult cases in the theory of truthmaking', *Monist* 83, 150–60.

Arrington, R. and H.-J. Glock (eds). 1996. *Wittgenstein and Quine.* London: Routledge.

Ayer, Alfred James. 1971. *Russell and Moore: The Analytical Heritage.* Cambridge, MA: Harvard University Press.

_____. 1972. *Bertrand Russell.* New York: Viking Press.

Bell, David and Neil Cooper (eds). 1990. *The Analytic Tradition: Meaning, Thought and Knowledge.* Oxford: Basil Blackwell.

Berghel, H., A. Hubner and E. Kohler (eds). 1979. *Wittgenstein, the Vienna Circle, and Critical Rationalism: Proceedings of the 3rd International Wittgenstein Symposium.* Vienna: Holder-Pichler-Tempsky.

Blackwell, Kenneth. 1968–69. 'The importance to philosophers of the Bertrand Russell Archive', *Dialogue* 7, 608–15.

_____. 1973. 'Our knowledge of our knowledge', *Russell*, no. 12, 11–13.

_____. 1974. 'Wittgenstein's impact on Russell's theory of belief', MA thesis, McMaster University.

_____. 1981. 'The early Wittgenstein and the middle Russell', in Block 1981, 1–30.

_____. 1989. 'Portrait of a philosopher of science', in Savage and Anderson 1989, 281–93.

Blackwell, Kenneth and E. R. Eames. 1975. 'Russell's unpublished book on theory of knowledge', *Russell*, no. 19, 3–14, 18.

Block, Irving (ed). 1981. *Perspectives on the Philosophy of Wittgenstein*. Oxford: Basil Blackwell.

Church, Alonzo. 1956. *Introduction to Mathematical Logic*, Vol. I. Princeton, NJ: Princeton University Press.

_____. 1976. 'Comparison of Russell's resolution of the semantical antinomies with that of Tarski', *Journal of Symbolic Logic* 41, 747–60.

Clark, Ronald W. 1975. *The Life of Bertrand Russell*. London: Jonathan Cape.

Cocchiarella, Nino. 1980. 'The development of the theory of logical types and the notion of a logical subject in Russell's early philosophy', *Synthese* 45, 71–115.

_____. 1987. *Logical Studies in Early Analytic Philosophy*. Columbus, OH: Ohio State University Press.

Copi, Irving M. 1971. *Theory of Logical Types*. London: Routledge & Kegan Paul.

Costello, Harry. 1957a. 'Logic in 1914 and now', *Journal of Philosophy* 54, 245–63.

_____. 1957b. 'Introduction to Ludwig Wittgenstein's "Notes on Logic, September, 1913"', *Journal of Philosophy* 54, 230–31.

Demos, Raphael. 1917. 'Discussion of a certain type of negative proposition', *Mind* 26, 188–96.

Diamond, Cora. 1988. 'Throwing away the ladder', *Philosophy* 63, 5–27.

_____. 1996. 'Wittgenstein, mathematics and ethics: resisting the attractions of realism', in Sluga and Stern 1996, 226–60.

Dorward, Alan. 1951. *Bertrand Russell: A Short Guide to His Philosophy*. London: Longmans, Green, and Co.

Dreben, Burton. 1996. 'Quine and Wittgenstein: the odd couple', in Arrington and Glock, 1996, 39–61.

_____ and Jean van Heijenoort. 1986. 'Introductory note to Gödel's completeness paper', in Gödel 1986.

_____ and Juliet Floyd. 1991. 'Tautology: on how not to use a word', *Synthese* 87, 23–49.

Eames, Elizabeth Ramsden. 1975. 'Philip E. B. Jourdain and the Open Court papers', *Carbondale* 2, 101–12.

_____. 1980. 'Response to Mr. Perkins', *Russell*, nos 35–36, 41–42.

_____. 1989. *Bertrand Russell's Dialogue with His Contemporaries*. Carbondale and Edwardsville, IL: Southern Illinois University Press.

Evans, Garth and John McDowell (eds). 1976. *Truth and Meaning: Essays in Semantics*. Oxford: Clarendon Press.

Floyd, Juliet. 1991. 'Wittgenstein on 2, 2, 2 . . . : the opening of Remarks on the Foundations of Mathematics', *Synthese* 87, 143–80.

_____. 1995. 'On saying what you really want to say: Wittgenstein, Gödel, and the trisection of the angle', in Hintikka 1995a, 373–426.

_____. 1998. 'The uncaptive eye: solipsism in Wittgenstein's *Tractatus*', in *Loneliness*, ed. L. Rouner, 79–108. Notre Dame, IN: Notre Dame University Press.

Frege, Gottlob. 1979. *Posthumous Writings*. Eds Gottfried Gabriel, Hans Hermes and Friedrich Kaulbach, trans. Peter Long and Roger White. Chicago: University of Chicago Press.

_____. 1980. *Philosophical and Mathematical Correspondence*. Eds Gottfried Gabriel, Hans Hermes, Friedrich Kambartel, Christien Thiel, Albert Veraart, abridged from the German edition by Brian McGuinness, trans. Hans Kaal. Chicago: University of Chicago Press.

French, Peter, Theodore Uehling, Jr. and Howard Wettstein (eds). 1981. *Foundations of Analytic Philosophy*, Midwest Studies in Philosophy, Vol. 6. Minneapolis: University of Minnesota Press.

Friedlander, Eli. 1992. 'Expressions of judgement: statute of limitation', Diss., Harvard University.

Geach, Peter. 1957. *Mental Acts*. London: Routledge & Kegan Paul.

Glock, Hans-Johann (ed.). 1997. *The Rise of Analytic Philosophy*. Oxford: Blackwell.

Gödel, Kurt. 1944. 'Russell's mathematical logic', in Schilpp 1944, 123–53.

_____. 1986. *Collected Works*, Vol. I. Eds S. Feiferman et al. New York: Oxford University Press.

Goldfarb, Warren. 1979. 'Logic in the twenties: the nature of the quantifier', *Journal of Symbolic Logic* 44, 351–68.

_____. 1983. 'I want you to bring me a slab: remarks on the opening sections of the *Philosophical Investigations*', *Synthese* 56, 265–82.

_____. 1989. 'Russell's reasons for ramification', in Savage and Anderson 1989, 24–40.

Gould, C. C. and Robert S. Cohen (eds). 1994. *Artifacts, Representations, and Social Practice*. Dordrecht: Kluwer.

Grattan-Guinness, I. 1974. 'The Russell Archives: some new light on Russell's logicism', *Annals of Science* 31, 387–406.

_____. 1977. *Dear Russell, Dear Jourdain: A Commentary on Russell's Logic,*

Based on His Correspondence with Philip Jourdain. New York: Columbia University Press.

_____. 1979. 'On Russell's logicism and its influence, 1910–1930', in Berghel, Hubner and Kohler, 1979, 275–80.

Griffin, Nicholas. 1980. 'Russell on the nature of logic (1903–1913)', *Synthese* 45, 117–88.

_____. 1985. 'Russell's multiple-relation theory of judgement', *Philosophical Studies* 47, 213–48.

_____. 1986. 'Wittgenstein's criticism of Russell's theory of judgement', *Russell* 5 (2), 132–45.

_____ (ed.). 2003. *The Cambridge Companion to Bertrand Russell*. Cambridge: Cambridge University Press.

Grossmann, Reinhardt. 1998. 'Wittgenstein and the problem of non-existent states of affairs', *Acta Analytica* 21, 139–46.

Haaparanta, L. and J. Hintikka (eds). 1986. *Frege Synthesized*. Dordrecht: D. Reidel.

Hacker, P. M. S. 1986. *Insight and Illusion: Themes in the Philosophy of Wittgenstein*. New York: Oxford University Press.

Haller, Rudolf and W. Grassl (eds). 1980. *Language, Logic, and Philosophy: Proceedings of the 4th International Wittgenstein Symposium*. Vienna: Holder-Pichler-Tempsky.

Hanks, P. W. (forthcoming). 'Wittgenstein's objection to Russell's multiple relation theory of judgement', *Synthese*.

Hintikka, Jaakko. 1988. 'On the development of the model-theoretic viewpoint in logical theory', *Synthese* 77, 1–36.

_____. 1994. 'An anatomy of Wittgenstein's picture theory', in Gould and Cohen 1994, 223–56.

_____ (ed). 1995a. *From Dedekind to Gödel: Essays on the Development of the Foundations of Mathematics*. Dordrecht: Kluwer.

_____. 1995b. 'Standard vs. nonstandard distinction: a watershed in the foundations of mathematics', in Hintikka 1995a, 21–44.

Hintikka, Jaakko and Gabriel Sandu. 1992. 'The skeleton in Frege's cupboard: the standard versus the nonstandard distinction', *Journal of Philosophy* 89, 290–315.

Hintikka, Merrill B. and Jaakko Hintikka. 1986. *Investigating Wittgenstein*. Oxford: Basil Blackwell.

Hylton, Peter. 1980. 'Russell's substitutional theory', *Synthese* 45, 1–31.

_____. 1984. 'The nature of the proposition and the revolt against idealism', in Rorty et al. 1984, 375–97.

_____. 1989. 'The significance of "On Denoting"', in Savage and Anderson 1989, 88–107.

_____. 1990a. 'Logic in Russell's logicism', in Bell and Cooper 1990, 137–72.

_____. 1990b. *Russell, Idealism and the Emergence of Analytic Philosophy*. Oxford: Clarendon Press.

_____. 1993. 'Functions and propositional functions in *Principia Mathematica*', in Irvine and Wedeking 1993, 342–60.

Irvine, A. D. and G. A. Wedeking (eds). 1993. *Russell and Analytic Philosophy*. Toronto: University of Toronto Press.

Isheguro, Hide. 1981. 'Wittgenstein and the theory of types', in Block 1981, 43–59.

Kenny, Anthony. 1973. *Wittgenstein*. Cambridge, MA: Harvard University Press.

Kilmister, C. W. 1984. *Russell*. New York: St. Martin's Press.

Kline, Morris. 1980. *Mathematics: The Loss of Certainty*. New York: Oxford University Press.

Kremer, Michael. 1997. 'Contextualism and holism in the early Wittgenstein: from *Prototractatus* to *Tractatus*', *Philosophical Topics* 25 (2), 87–120.

Kripke, Saul. 1976. 'Is there a problem with substitutional quantification?' in Evans and McDowell 1976, 324–419.

Lackey, Douglas. 1981. 'Russell's 1913 map of the mind', in French, Uehling and Wettstein 1981, 125–42.

Landini, Gregory. 1991. 'A new interpretation of Russell's multiple relation theory of judgement', *History and Philosophy of Logic* 12, 37–69.

_____. 1993. 'Reconciling PM's ramified type theory with the doctrine of the unrestricted variable of *The Principles*', in Irvine and Wedeking 1993, 361–94.

Linsky, Bernard. 2003. 'The metaphysics of Logical Atomism', in Griffin 2003, 371–91.

Malcolm, Norman. 1984. *Ludwig Wittgenstein: A Memoir*, 2nd edn, with a biographical sketch by Georg Henrik von Wright and Wittgenstein's letters to Malcolm. London: Oxford University Press.

McGuinness, Brian. 1972. 'Bertrand Russell and Ludwig Wittgenstein's "Notes on Logic"', *Revue Internationale de Philosophie* 26, 444–60.

_____. 1974. 'The *Grundgedanke* of the *Tractatus*', in Vesey 1974, 48–61.

_____ (ed.). 1979. *Wittgenstein and the Vienna Circle: Conversations Recorded by Friedrich Waismann*, trans. Joachim Schulte and Brian McGuinness. Oxford: Basil Blackwell.

_____. 1988. *Wittgenstein: A Life, Young Ludwig 1889–1921*. Berkeley and Los Angeles: University of California Press.

Monk, Ray. 1996. *Bertrand Russell: The Spirit of Solitude, 1872–1921*. New York: The Free Press.

_____. 1997. 'Was Russell an analytical philosopher?' in Glock 1997, 35–50.

_____. 1990. *Ludwig Wittgenstein: The Duty of Genius*. New York: Penguin.

Moore, G. E. 1922. *Philosophical Studies*. London: Routledge & Kegan Paul.

_____. 1954–55. 'Wittgenstein's lectures in 1930–1933', *Mind* 63, 64 (nos 249, 251, 253), 1–15, 289–316, 1–27. Reprinted in Ammerman 1965, 233–84.

_____. 1992. *Lectures on Metaphysics, 1934–1935, from the notes of Alice Ambrose and Margaret MacDonald*, ed. Alice Ambrose. New York: Peter Lang.

Oaklander, L. Nathan and Silvano Miracchi. 1980. 'Russell, negative facts, and ontology', *Philosophy of Science* 47, 434–55.

Parker, Dewitt. 1945. 'Knowledge by acquaintance', *Philosophical Review* 54, 1–18.

Patterson, Wayne A. 1993. *Bertrand Russell's Philosophy of Logical Atomism.* New York: Peter Lang.

_____. 1996. 'The logical structure of Russell's negative facts', *Russell: The Journal of the Bertrand Russell Archives*, new series, 16 (1), 45–66.

Peacocke, Christopher. 1976. 'What is a logical constant?' *Journal of Philosophy* 73 (9), 221–41.

Pears, David. 1967. *Bertrand Russell and the British Tradition in Philosophy.* London: Fontana Press.

_____. (ed.), 1972. *Bertrand Russell: A Collection of Critical Essays.* Garden City, NY: Anchor Books.

_____. 1975a. *Questions in the Philosophy of Mind.* London: Duckworth.

_____. 1975b. 'Russell's theories of memory', in Pears 1975a, 224–50.

_____. 1975c. 'Wittgenstein's treatment of solipsism in the Tractatus', in Pears 1975a, 272–92.

_____. 1977. 'The relation between Wittgenstein's picture theory of propositions and Russell's theories of judgement', *Philosophical Review* 86, 177–96.

_____. 1979. 'Wittgenstein's picture theory and Russell's *Theory of Knowledge*', in Berghel, Hubner and Kohler 1979, 101–7.

_____. 1981a. 'The function of acquaintance in Russell's philosophy', *Synthese* 46, 149–66.

_____. 1981b. 'The logical independence of elementary propositions', in Block 1981, 74–84.

_____ (ed.). 1985. *Philosophy of Logical Atomism*, with an intro. by D. Pears. La Salle, IL: Open Court.

_____. 1987. *The False Prison: A Study of the Development of Wittgenstein's Philosophy.* New York: Oxford University Press.

_____. 1989. 'Russell's 1913 *Theory of Knowledge* manuscript', in Savage and Anderson 1989, 169–82.

Perkins, Jr., R. K. 1979. 'Russell's unpublished book on theory of knowledge', *Russell*, nos 35–36, 37–40.

Pritchard, H. R. 1915. 'Mr. Bertrand Russell on *Our Knowledge of the External World*', *Mind* 24, 1–40.

Quine, W. V. 1956. 'Quantifiers and propositional attitudes', *Journal of Philosophy* 53 (5), 177–87. Reprinted in Quine 1976, 185–96.

_____. 1966. 'Russell's ontological development', *Journal of Philosophy* 63 (21), 657–67. Reprinted in Quine 1981, 73–85.

_____. 1969. *Set Theory and its Logic*, rev. edn. Cambridge, MA: Harvard University Press.

_____. 1976. *Ways of Paradox and Other Essays*, rev. and enlarged edn. Cambridge, MA: Harvard University Press.

_____. 1981. *Theories and Things*. Cambridge, MA: Harvard University Press.

Ramsey, Frank. P. 1990. *Philosophical Papers*. Ed. D. H. Mellor. Cambridge: Cambridge University Press.

Rhees, Rush. 1974. 'Questions on logical inference', in Vesey 1974.

Ricketts, Thomas. 1985. 'Frege, the *Tractatus*, and the logocentric predicament', *Nous* 19 (1), 3–15.

_____. 1986a. 'Generality, meaning, and sense in Frege', *Pacific Philosophical Quarterly* 67 (3), 172–95.

_____. 1986b. 'Objectivity and objecthood: Frege's metaphysics of judgement', in Haaparanta and Hintikka 1986, 65–95.

_____. 1996. 'Pictures, logic, and the limits of sense in Wittgenstein's *Tractatus*', in Sluga and Stern 1996, 59–99.

Roberts, George W. (ed). 1979. *Bertrand Russell Memorial Volume*. London: George Allen & Unwin.

Rorty, R., J. B. Schneewind and Q. Skinner (eds). 1984. *Philosophy in History: Essays on the Historiography of Philosophy*. Cambridge: Cambridge University Press.

Rosenberg, Jay F. 1972. 'Russell on negative facts', *Nous* 6, 27–40.

Sainsbury, R. M. 1979. *Russell*. London: Routledge & Kegan Paul.

Savage, C. Wade and C. Anthony Anderson (eds). 1989. *Rereading Russell: Essays on Bertrand Russell's Metaphysics and Epistemology*. Minnesota Studies in the Philosophy of Science, 12. Minneapolis: University of Minnesota Press.

Schilpp, Paul Arthur (ed.). 1944. *The Philosophy of Bertrand Russell*. The Library of Living Philosophers, 5. Chicago: Northwestern University (4th edn, La Salle, IL: Open Court, 1971).

Sluga, H., and D. Stern (eds). 1996. *Cambridge Companion to Wittgenstein*. Cambridge: Cambridge University Press.

Sommerville, S. T. 1979. 'Types, categories and significance', Diss., McMaster University.

_____. 1980. 'Wittgenstein to Russell (July, 1913): "I am very sorry to hear

. . . my objection paralyzes you"', in Haller and Grassl 1980, 62–75.

Stevens, Graham. 2003. 'Re-examining Russell's paralysis: ramified type-theory and Wittgenstein's objection to Russell's theory of judgement', *Russell: The Journal of the Bertrand Russell Archives*, new series, no. 23, 5–26.

_____. 2004. 'From Russell's Paradox to the theory of judgement: Wittgenstein and Russell on the unity of the proposition', *Theoria* 70, 28–61.

_____. 2005. *The Russellian Origins of Analytical Philosophy: Bertrand Russell and the Unity of the Proposition*. London: Routledge.

_____. 2006. 'Russell's re-psychologising of the proposition', *Synthese*, 151, 1 (July), 99–124.

Stock, Guy. 1974. 'Wittgenstein on Russell's "Theory of Judgement"', in Vesey 1974, 63–75.

Stout, G. F. 1930. *Philosophy and Psychology*. London: Macmillan.

_____ (ed.). 1967a. *From Frege to Gödel: A Sourcebook in Mathematical Logic, 1879–1931*. Cambridge, MA: Harvard University Press.

van Heijenoort, Jean. 1967b. 'Logic as calculus and logic as language', *Synthese*, 17, 324–30.

Vesey, Godfrey (ed.). 1974. *Understanding Wittgenstein*. London: Macmillan.

Wahl, Russell. 1986. 'Bertrand Russell's theory of judgement', *Synthese* 68, 383–407.

Wang, Hao. 1988. *Beyond Analytic Philosophy: Doing Justice to What We Know*. Cambridge, MA: MIT Press.

White, Alan R. 1979. 'Belief as a propositional attitude', in Roberts 1979, 242–63.

White, R. M. 1974. 'Can whether one proposition makes sense depend on the truth of another? (*Tractatus* 2.0211-2)', in Vesey 1974, 15–29.

Index

acquaintance 5
analysis 72–4, 77
attention 28, 35

belief
  asymmetrical relations 84–5, 86
  certainty 91–2
  cognition 17
  corresponding complex 83–4, 85
  disbelief 82–3
  eliminating 107, 109, 112
  facts 99–101, 106
  false 20–3, 29, 41, 45, 46, 47, 57–8,
    61, 71, 86
  knowledge 87–8
  logical form 66
  memory 91
  and molecular forms 8
  and multiple relation theory 6–7,
    20–3, 26, 33–7, 41
  non-spatial 95, 102–6, 109
  and perception 33, 35–6
  psychology 17–18, 42
  scepticism 89
  truth 83
Blackwell, Kenneth 45, 61

classes
  paradoxes 19–20
  and theory of incomplete symbols
    15–16, 19
complexes
  analysis 72
  atomic 40, 81
  conjunction 49–50
  corresponding 83–4, 85, 88–9
  form 54, 55–6, 59

molecular 80
negative 97
non-existent 37–8, 40
  perception of 87
positive 97
sense 51–2
types 60
concepts 13–15
consciousness see mind

data 4, 27–8, 35–6, 45, 53, 54, 68,
  77, 86
Demos, Raphael 82
denoting 13–17, 42, 49, 51, 99
depiction 68, 102–4
descriptions, theory of 14–16, 27,
  90–1
dualism 4, 8, 63, 67, 90, 109

Eames, Elizabeth Ramsden 44, 45,
  59, 61
epistemology 1, 11, 19, 30, 38, 47,
  62, 68, 69, 73, 76, 78–9, 96, 107,
  111, 112
ethics 90
evolutionary psychology 53, 56
experience
  analysis of 4–5
extensionalism 105

facts
  atomic 108
  complexes 52
  corresponding 83, 87
  empirical 76
  judging 61, 66–7
  mental 67

negative   18, 82–3, 96, 97–9, 102,
    103, 106
neutral   98–101
positive   97, 98, 102, 103
and propositions   7, 52–3, 94–5
structure   64–7
as things   73
and understanding   102–3
falsehood   11, 82
form   7, 34, 37–8, 42–6, 48–50, 53–6,
    57–61, 70–1, 77, 79, 92–3, 95,
    98, 112
Frege, Gottlob   53
functions, propositional   19, 30

Gestalt psychology   53, 55
Griffin, Nicholas   40, 45, 110

Hanks, P. W.   110, 111

idealism   17–18, 57, 89
inference   5
intentionalism   8

James, William   84
judgement
  analysis   72–4, 76
  analytic   88–9
  asymmetrical relations   52, 56–9,
      80–1, 84–5
  elementary   30–1, 42
  facts   99–101
  false   32, 57, 69, 70
  general   31, 42
  logical relations   105
  multiple relation theory   1–2, 6,
      11–13, 16, 23–6, 31–7, 41, 45,
      46, 73, 77, 89, 92, 95, 109–12
  neutral facts   98–101
  perception   28–9, 74–5
  propositions   12–13, 81
  self-evident   87–91, 93
  theory of incomplete symbols   16
  types   110–11
knowledge by acquaintance   18,
    27–8, 36, 42, 47, 90–1

language
  metaphysics   9–10
logic
  belief   66
  constants   48, 54, 57, 81, 104
  data   53, 54, 68, 77
  denoting   14
  and epistemology   107–8, 112
  form   37–8, 42–4, 54
  general truths   12
  perception   71, 75
  propositions   16, 62, 69, 77–9
  subject   67
  types   30, 42, 110–11

McGuinness, Brian   108–9
mathematics   63, 90
meaning
  atomistic doctrine   8, 12, 27, 68,
      76, 96, 112
  and denoting   14–16
  truth conditions   105
Meinong, Alexius   6, 17, 18, 20, 41,
    42, 95
metaphysics   9, 111
mind
  perception and judgement   28–9
  psychology   17
  truth   7
Morrell, Ottoline   2–3, 7–9, 37, 43,
    61–2, 69, 71, 81, 92, 113

names   27, 30, 36, 51–2, 67, 68, 73,
    74, 75–6, 84
neutral monism   63, 84, 90, 109

paradoxes
  beliefs as individual   22
  Liar   6, 19–20, 21–3
  propositions   17, 19–20, 42
  vicious circle doctrine   30
Pears, David   36
perception   8, 27, 28–9, 33, 35, 52,
    71, 72–5, 78, 84, 85–6, 91, 97
philosophy
  activity not doctrine   89–90
  logical   1

as pseudo-science 114
scientific 113
pragmatism 25–6
predicates 53–4
properties *see* predicates
propositions
  analysis 54, 76
  asymmetrical relations 80, 85, 100
  atomic 5, 7, 69, 81, 86, 108–9
  belief 17, 20–3, 108
  bipolarity 43, 70–1, 72, 81, 94–5,
    96, 102, 103–4, 106, 109
  and concepts 13–15
  conjunction 86
  epistemology 62
  and facts 7, 94
  false 20, 21, 24, 37, 41, 80
  form 42–6
  general 77–8, 79
  generating 5
  imbedded 52–3
  and judgement 12–13, 81
  logic 62, 77, 78
  molecular 5, 7, 20, 59, 69, 81
  negative 18, 82–3
  objective 13, 24, 33, 41, 43, 68, 71,
    87
  paradoxes 17, 19–20, 42
  and psychological acts 8–9, 17–19
  relations between constituents 92
  sense 96, 101, 102, 104–5, 107
  significance 110
  and solipsism 91
  substitution 38–9
  symbolism 39–40
  types 30
  true and false 24, 41, 111
  truth conditions 105–6
  understanding 62–7, 97–8
  verification 85, 100, 102
psychology
  descriptive 17–19
  evolutionary 53, 56
  Gestalt 53, 55
  logic and epistemology 108
  propositions 8–9, 17, 20
  sense 63

Ramsay, Frank P. 23
relations 48–52, 61, 67, 68, 71–2, 78,
    79–80, 92–3, 94–5, 103
Russell, Bertrand
  'Knowledge by Acquaintance and
    Knowledge by Description', 47
  lectures on logical atomism (1918)
    101–2, 106
  letters to Ottoline Morrell 2–3,
    7–9, 37, 43, 61–2, 69, 71, 81, 90,
    92, 94, 113
  'Meinong's Theory of Complexes
    and Assumptions' 17
  'On Denoting' (1905) 14–17, 21
  'On the Nature of Truth and
    Falsehood' 21–2, 25, 32
  'On the Relation of Universals and
    Particulars', 53
  Our Knowledge of the External World
    108–9
  'Paradox of the Liar' 20–1, 22–3
  Philosophy of Logical Atomism 66
  Principia Mathematica 1, 28, 30, 73,
    87–8, 110
  Principles of Mathematics 13–14,
    18–19, 49
  Problems of Philosophy 29, 47, 88
  'Props' (1913) 95–6, 102–6
  Theory of Knowledge 1–2, 3–6, 7–10,
    23, 26–7, 29, 33, 38, 40–1, 43–6,
    49–52, 61, 62, 65–7, 71, 73–4,
    82, 86, 94–102, 103, 105, 107,
    109, 110–12
  'Types' 20, 21, 22
  'What is Logic?' 37–8, 45, 49, 62
  see also Wittgenstein

scepticism 29, 71, 89, 90–1
self
  absence of 106
  relation to proposition 12, 13
sense 31–3, 37, 43, 47–8, 51–2, 56,
    58, 63–4, 69, 78, 96, 101, 104
sentences
  atomic 53
  belief 41
  form 70

identity criteria 49
meaning 8, 76
molecular 53, 55
theory of incomplete symbols 16,
    42
understanding 55, 56, 68
verification 12
sequence 51
similarity 64–6
solipsism 71, 90–1
Sommerville, S. T. 40, 59–60, 110–11
Stout, G. F. 32
substitution 38–9
symbolism 39–40, 102–6

theory of incomplete symbols 6,
    12–16, 19, 21, 37, 41, 42, 62–3
thought
  atomic 91–2
  molecular 92
truth
  belief 83, 85
  correspondence 25, 26–7, 29, 71,
      87, 95
  corresponding complex 83–5
  elementary judgements 30–1
  and falsehood 23–4, 82
  general judgements 31
  and incomplete symbols 15
  and knowledge 11, 75
  logical propositions 12
  mathematics 63

and mind 7
naming of complexes 52–3
neutral facts 100
perception 29
pragmatism 25–6
propositions 105–6
self-evident beliefs 87–8
types, theory of 30, 39, 42, 110–11

understanding 62–9, 73, 77–81, 92,
    96–8, 102–3

verbs 13, 24, 101–2
verification 12, 76, 83, 84–5, 100,
    102

Wittgenstein, Ludwig
  letters to Russell
    (January 1913) 38–40
    (June 1913) 6, 7, 107, 109,
        111–12, 113
  Notebooks 46
  'Notes on Logic' 53, 61, 87, 104,
      108
  Tractatus Logico-Philosophicus 9, 74,
      86, 109, 114
  visits Russell
    (20 May 1913) 6, 7, 44, 57–8, 60,
        61, 68, 69, 70, 92, 101
    (26 May 1913) 6, 7, 67, 92, 96,
        109
words 53–4, 56, 68